I0095748

Hans Karl Peterlini, Jasmin Donlic (eds.)
Jahrbuch Migration und Gesellschaft/
Yearbook Migration and Society 2022/2023

The series is edited by Hans Karl Peterlini and Jasmin Donlic.

Hans Karl Peterlini (Prof. Dr.) is a professor at the Department of Educational Science at Alpen-Adria-Universität Klagenfurt, Austria, working in the fields of general pedagogy and diversity education, as well as peace research and peace education. His research interests are personal and social learning processes in schools and lifeworlds, experiences of living together in migration societies, and between majorities and minorities.

Jasmin Donlic (Dr.) is an assistant professor at the Department of Educational Science at Alpen-Adria-Universität Klagenfurt, Austria (working unit for general pedagogy and diversity education). His main research interests are postmigration, diversity and education and qualitative research methods (grounded theory and participatory research).

Hans Karl Peterlini, Jasmin Donlic (eds.)

Jahrbuch Migration und Gesellschaft/
Yearbook Migration and Society 2022/2023

»Climate«

[transcript]

The editors acknowledge the financial support by the University of Klagenfurt and its Faculty of Arts, Humanities & Education.

ALPEN-ADRIA
UNIVERSITÄT
KLAGENFURT

KUBI
@aau.at

Supported by the Unesco Chair "Global Citizenship Education - Culture of Diversity and Peace" at the University of Klagenfurt.

UNESCO
uni Twin

United Nations
Educational, Scientific and
Cultural Organization

UNESCO Chair on Global
Citizenship Education,
Culture of Diversity and Peace
University of Klagenfurt, Austria

Each paper was reviewed in a double-blind peer-review process. The editors thank the national and international reviewers for the quality assurance of the publication.

Bibliographic information published by the Deutsche Nationalbibliothek
The Deutsche Nationalbibliothek lists this publication in the Deutsche Nationalbibliografie; detailed bibliographic data are available in the Internet at http://dnb.d-nb.de

First published in 2023 by transcript Verlag, Bielefeld
© **Hans Karl Peterlini, Jasmin Donlic (eds.)**

Cover layout: Maria Arndt, Bielefeld
Typeset: Christian Herzog

Print-ISBN 978-3-8376-6657-1
PDF-ISBN 978-3-8394-6657-5
https://doi.org/10.14361/9783839466575
ISSN of series: 2700-6824
eISSN of series: 2703-0547

Contents

Klima – eine Frage von Globaler Verantwortung und Citizenship / Climate—a Question of Global Responsibility and Citizenship
Ein einleitender Kommentar / An Introductory Commentary

Hans Karl Peterlini, Jasmin Donlic

Wenn es eines letzten Nachweises bedurft hätte, dass die problematisch ver-einfachende, in politischen Diskursen gleichwohl ungehemmt florierende Push-Pull-Theorie (vgl. Lee 1966; 1972) der Komplexität von Migration nicht gerecht wird, dann liegt dieser spätestens mit dem kaum entwirrbaren Zusammenhang von Klimawandel und Fluchtmigration vor. Die mit dem Push-Poll-Modell einhergehende „trennscharfe Unterscheidung zwischen freiwilligen und erzwungenen Migrationsprozessen" (vgl. Klein 2022) er-laubt vielfache jene Diskurse, die Flucht und Migration dadurch zu steuern versuchen, dass die Push-Faktoren vorgeblich gutmeinend vermindert und die Pull-Faktoren zynisch verschlechtert werden. So erklärte erst am 31. März 2023 der österreichische Bundeskanzler Karl Nehammer, dass er die Sozialleistungen für Zugewanderte in den ersten fünf Jahren kürzen wolle, um Österreich nach dem Vorbild von Dänemark für geflüchtete Menschen „möglichst unattraktiv" zu machen (ORF.at 2023). Von einer Politik, die ver-hindern will, dass Österreich ein „Zuwanderungsland ins Sozialsystem" (ebd.) werde, ist es nur ein Schritt zum „Überforderungsnarrativ in Kombi-nation mit dem Bedrohungsnarrativ", das nach einer Studie der Friedrich-Ebert-Stiftung nicht mehr allein in den Reden von AfD-Abgeordneten im deutschen Bundestag dominiert (Klein 2022).

Push und Pull versagen als Erkenntniskategorien in Bezug auf den Zusammenhang von Klima, Klimawandel und Migration. Sie ermöglichen kein Abschieben von Verantwortung auf Herkunftsländer und entlarven jene Narrative als Selbsttäuschung, wonach es genügen würde, ungewünschte Menschen aus dem Globalen Süden fernzuhalten, um die eigene heile Welt zu schützen. Diese wird nicht von Migration bedroht, im Gegenteil, sondern von den bisher schadlos auf den Rest der Welt abgeladenen und nun wie ein Bumerang zurückkommenden Folgen imperialer Lebensweisen (vgl. Lessenich 2016; Brand/Wissen 2017). Zugleich werden an der durch die kritische Migrationsforschung längst vollzogenen Entzauberung des Push-Pull-Modells auch herkömmliche Lösungsmodelle brüchig. Der Klimawandel lässt sich weder mit Interventionen im Sinne einer „Bleibeperspektive" in den Griff kriegen noch mit verschärftem Grenzmanagement oder gar Zäunen, wie sie nicht mehr nur von rechtspopulistischen Regierungen (von der Trump-Regierung an der Grenze zu Mexiko, von der Orban-Regierung in Ungarn) zur Abhaltung von Menschen erwogen und teilweise durchgeführt wurden (vgl. Römhild et al. 2021).

Ein gleich anschauliches wie schwieriges Beispiel ist der im Zusammenhang von Klima und Migration vielfach thematisierte Inselstaat Kiribati. In den rund 30 verstreuten Inseln im Südpazifik sind die Folgen des Klimawandels, der in Europa noch an der Schneelage in den Skigebieten gemessen wird, auf existenzbedrohende Weise verdichtet. Die Inseln sind so klein, dass es praktisch gar kein Hinterland gibt, in das sich die Menschen angesichts des ansteigenden Meeresspiegels – seit Jahrzehnten um durchschnittlich 3,7 Millimeter pro Jahr – zurückziehen könnten. Das Leben findet hier überall an der Küste statt, da überall Küste ist. Die Inseln sind zunehmend heftigeren Sturmfluten ausgesetzt, die Süßwasserquellen drohen durch das Vorrücken des Meerwassers zu versalzen. Die Lebensbedingungen werden zunehmend schwieriger, der Lebensraum droht schlicht verlorenzugehen. Kiribati stellt einen Appell an eine Klima- und Migrationspolitik dar, die solche Szenarien nicht nur rhetorisch beschwört, sondern als Verpflichtung für globale Gerechtigkeit ernst nimmt. Ein Ansatz dazu könnte sein, Migration nicht länger losgelöst von Fragen einer Globalen Citizenship im Sinne eines globalen Daseinsrechts und globaler Verantwortung wahrzunehmen und geltend zu machen (vgl. Peterlini 2023: 184–190). Am Fall Kiribati greifen die in der Suche nach Anpassungsleistungen an den Klimawandel meist „sehr technisch geführten Debatten" (Klepp 2013: 415) zu kurz. Nicht nur, dass diese Maßnahmen bei ansteigendem Meeresspiegel im Zusammenwirken mit den Verschlechterungen der Lebensbedingungen nicht ausreichen könnten; sie tragen vielfach dem Wissen, den Erfahrungen, Bedürfnissen und eigenen Bewältigungskompetenzen der indigenen Bevölkerung nicht Rechnung: „Die pazifischen Inselstaaten werden als marginalisiert, vulnerabel und entwicklungsbedürftig sowie als klein, arm und nicht entwickelbar konzeptualisiert", fasst die Meeresforscherin Silja Klepp (ebd.: 416) ihre Einsichten zusammen. In solchen Zuschreibungen, die zugleich Schicksalshaftigkeit insinuieren, wirken koloniale Diskurse und epistemische Dominanzen weiter. Die alarmierenden medialen und politischen Narrative um die untergehenden Inseln tragen selbst dann, wenn sie gut gemeint sind, zu einer Narration der Aussichtslosigkeit und Hilflosigkeit bei, die global- und lokalpolitische Verantwortlichkeiten verschleiert. Die Situation dieser Inseln verlangt Antworten, die über punktuelle Interventionen und Hilfeleistungen hinausgehen. Sie nehmen zuallererst die Weltgemeinschaft – und da vor allem die industrialisierten Ökonomien – in eine globale Pflicht, bei der Reduktion von Emissionen von halbherzigen auf konsequente Maßnahmen umzuschalten, ein notwendiger politischer Paradigmenwechsel, der wohl vor allem deshalb gescheut wird, weil er nicht nur technische Implikationen hätte, sondern nach neuen Formen ökologisch verträglichen und global solidarischen Wirtschaftens verlangt. Damit hängt auch die unvermeidliche, aber weitgehend vermiedene Frage zusammen, wie schmerzhaft die Umstellungen der kapitalistischen Lebens- und Wirtschaftsformen sein müssen, um die viel tiefer klaffenden globalen Wunden vielleicht noch zu heilen.

Nicht minder tiefgreifend sind Fragen zum Verständnis von Migration, Citizenship, Partizipation und Demokratie. So erhob die Regierung Kiribatis schon vor Jahren die Forderung nach einem umfassenden Migrationsrecht für alle ihre Bürger*innen inklusive eines freien Zugangs zu Arbeits- und Bildungsmöglichkeiten in den Orten ihrer Wahl. Die selbst in Kiribati nicht unumstrittene und verstörende Vorstellung, dass die Weltgemeinschaft auch geschlossene Siedlungsräume für die Bevölkerung lebensunwert gewordener Inseln und Landstriche zur Verfügung stellen müsse, stellt auf einer prinzipiellen Ebene das Recht auf eine Staatsbürger*innenschaft weltweit dar. Dies trifft sich durchaus mit der visionären Konzeption Edgar Morins der Erde als Heimatland aller (vgl. Morin/Kern 1999; Kramer/Wintersteiner 2021). Zugleich kann eine solche Forderung auch so gelesen werden, dass die Inseln und ihre Bevölkerung schon aufgegeben sind und nur noch Asylplätze für die Klimaflüchtlinge gesucht werden müssen. Vorerst aber wird politisch überhaupt erst die Definition von „Klimaflüchtlingen" debattiert; die Betroffenen fallen nicht einmal unter die Genfer Flüchtlingskonvention und können keinen Status als Geflüchtete geltend machen.

Die existenzielle Not der Atolle im Südpazifik kann mit einem Denken in Nord-Süd-Kategorien nicht beantwortet werden. Sie besagt, auf einen einfachen Nenner gebracht, nichts anderes, als dass die Lebensbedingungen auf dieser Erde keine national teilbare, sondern eine globale Verantwortung darstellen, und zwar nicht nur klimatisch, sondern auch ökonomisch, sozial, völker- und individualrechtlich. Die Wahrnehmung dieser Verantwortung kann, im Sinne einer Global Citizenship, nicht von den dominanten Machtzentren aus gesteuert werden, sie muss einem fairen Aushandlungsprozess auf Augenhöhe anvertraut werden. Es genügt nicht mehr, und sei es in der Intention eines freilich hilflosen Helfens, über die bedrohten Gebiete zu reden, sondern es ist notwendig, sich mit den dort lebenden Menschen auseinanderzusetzen. Die gilt umso mehr für den machtvollen Diskurs von Migration als Anpassung, der in unterschiedlichen Nuancen auch in den Klimadebatten eine Rolle spielt. Lokale Anpassungsstrategien dienen vielfach dazu, sich nicht der globalen Tragweite stellen zu müssen und die Vulnerabilitäten, strukturellen Problematiken, Lebensnöte und Bewältigungskompetenzen der Menschen vor Ort zu relativieren.

Dass Fragen des Lebens und Überlebens danach entschieden werden, wer größere Macht, mehr Geld und potentere Waffen hat, stellt sich als Jahrhundertversagen der Industriestaaten heraus. Diese Selbstüberschätzung in einer Haltung der Bevormundung und Bereicherung ist gescheitert, denn mittlerweile ist niemand mehr sicher, auch jene nicht, die das Problem immer noch anderswo ausgelagert sehen wollen. Wie in einer innerstaatlichen Demokratie müssen auch global Machthabende dieselben Regeln einhalten wie alle Betroffenen und sich nicht über diese hinwegsetzen. Bei Fragen, die das Herz der Gemeinschaft und des Zusammenlebens betreffen wie etwa Verfassungsbestimmungen, gelten in soliden Demokratien besonders hohe Mehrheiten, um zu verhindern, dass einzelne Lobbys sich im Alleingang die Regeln richten können. In einer globalen Perspektive müsste das Vetorecht, das in den Vereinten Nationen nur die Supermächte haben, auf das kleinste Atoll übertragen werden, wenn es denn durch das Verhalten der anderen in seiner Existenz bedroht ist. In reifen und funktionierenden Demokratien, wie sie leider unter der Vorherrschaft von medialen und politischen Lobbys zunehmend erodieren, können Gerichte auch große Entscheidungen stoppen, wenn diese das Recht eines einzelnen oder einzelner Gruppen verletzen.

Migration ist nicht ein Problem in Folge des Klimawandels und anderer Missstände dieser Welt, sondern eine Möglichkeit, die Probleme der Erde neu und besser zu verstehen als globale Verantwortlichkeit. Dieser Verantwortung kann sich, ganz nüchtern und gar nicht visionär, niemand entziehen. Sie bedarf der Mitsprache aller ohne höhere und geringere Verteilung von Rechten. Das ist weder Utopie noch Unmöglichkeit: Alles andere wäre vielmehr ein Festhalten an der dystopischen Verfasstheit unserer Gegenwart.

Global Citizenship bedeutet in diesem Sinne sowohl eine Definition personalen Existenzrechts und politischer Souveränität unabhängig von der Größe und Machtausstattung eines politischen Subjekts als auch eine Entnationalisierung von Recht und Zugehörigkeit. Menschen müssen, unabhängig davon, woher sie kommen und wohin sie gehen, überall auf dieser Welt ein Recht auf Dasein und Teilhabe haben. Eher als eine Utopie zu sein, entspricht eine solche Forderung jener „unmöglichen Möglichkeit", die Derrida einfordert, nämlich „durch das Sprechen sich etwas ereignen zu lassen" (Derrida 2003: 24).

Mit dieser Ausgabe des Jahrbuchs Migration und Gesellschaft möchten wir zu einem solchen Sprechen beitragen. Die umfassende Thematik lässt sich auf den Seiten eines Buches nur ansatzweise, an einzelnen theoretischen Zugriffen und konkreten Beispielen darstellen. Durch den Versuch, Klimaforschung aus unterschiedlichen wissenschaftlichen Perspektiven mit einer kritischen und reflexiven Migrationsforschung in einen Dialog zu bringen, treffen in diesem Band auch unterschiedliche Wissenschaftskulturen aufeinander, die – wie auch die Reviews da und dort zeigten – nicht immer ganz zueinander fanden; wir fanden es in einigen wenigen Fällen für wichtig, auch hier nicht „Anpassung" einzufordern und auch unterschiedliche Verständnisse nebeneinander stehen zu lassen. Wir hoffen damit zu einem wissenschaftlichen Diskurs beizutragen, der aus der Thematisierung von Migration und Weltgesellschaft seine Impulse und Potenziale bezieht, um komplexe Zusammenhänge besser zu verstehen. Wir danken allen Autor*innen und Reviewer*innen, die zu diesem Jahrbuch beigetragen haben.

If final proof were needed that push-pull theory (cf. Lee 1966; 1972), which is problematically simplifying yet flourishes unchecked in political discourses, does not do justice to the complexity of migration, then this comes at the latest in the form of the almost unfathomable connection between climate change and refugee migration. The "sharp distinction between voluntary and forced migration processes" (cf. Klein 2022) that the push-pull model entails permits the existence of various discourses that attempt to control flight and migration by diminishing the push factors (supposedly with good intentions) and cynically lowering the pull factors. For example, as recently as March 31, 2023, the Austrian Chancellor Karl Nehammer declared that he wanted to cut social benefits for immigrants in the first five years in order to make Austria "as unattractive as possible" for refugees, following the example of Denmark (ORF.at 2023). From a policy designed to prevent Austria from becoming a "country of immigration into the social system" (ibid.), it is only a step to the "narrative of being overwhelmed combined with the narrative of threat" that, according to a study by the Friedrich Ebert Foundation, dominates more than just the speeches of right-wing AfD members of the German Bundestag (Klein 2022).

Push and pull fail as categories of knowledge with regard to the connection between climate, climate change and migration. They do not allow responsibility to be shifted to immigrants' countries of origin, and they expose as self-delusion those narratives claiming that to protect our own, unspoilt world, all we have to do is keep out unwanted people from the Global South. That unspoilt world is not threatened by migration: on the contrary, it is the consequences of imperialist ways of life that have so far been dumped without a care on the rest of the world and are now coming back like a boomerang (cf. Lessenich 2016; Brand & Wissen 2017). At the same time, the disillusionment with the push-pull model that has long since been accomplished by critical migration research also renders conventional solutions fragile. Climate change can neither be tackled with interventions such as offering immigrants a good chance of being granted leave to stay, nor with tightened border management or even fences to keep people out, as considered and sometimes implemented not only by right-wing populist governments (the Trump administration between the USA and Mexico, the Orban government in Hungary) (cf. Römhild et al. 2021).

An equally illustrative and difficult example is the island nation of Kiribati, which has been the subject of much discussion in connection with the climate and migration. While the consequences of climate change are still measured in Europe in terms of snow levels in ski resorts, they are focused in a manner that threatens the very existence of the people in the 30 or so scattered islands in the South Pacific. The islands are so small that there is practically nowhere for people to retreat from sea levels that have been rising by an average of 3.7 millimeters per year for decades. Life here always takes place on the coast, because everywhere is coast. The islands are exposed to increasingly violent storm surges, and sources of fresh water are in danger of becoming saline as seawater advances. Living conditions are becoming increasingly difficult; people's habitat is threatening to simply vanish. Kiribati calls for a climate and migration policy that does not merely invoke such scenarios rhetorically, but takes them seriously as a commitment to global justice. One approach to this could be to stop viewing and treating migration as unrelated to the discussion on global citizenship, i.e. a global right to exist and global responsibility (cf. Peterlini 2023: 184–190). The usually "very technical" (Klepp 2013: 415) debates on finding ways to adapt to climate change fall short when it comes to Kiribati. It is not just that these measures might not be enough to tackle rising sea levels in combination with the deterioration of living conditions; often, they also do not take into account the indigenous population's own knowledge, experiences, needs and coping skills. As marine researcher Silja Klepp (ibid.: 416) puts it, summing up her insights, "Pacific island states are conceptualized as marginalized, vulnerable, and in need of development, as well as being small, poor, and incapable of development." Labels of this kind, with their fatalist insinuations, show that colonial discourses and forms of epistemic dominance are still at work. Even when well-intentioned, the alarmist narratives in the media and politics surrounding the sinking islands contribute to a narrative of hopelessness and helplessness that obscures global and local political responsibilities. The situation of these islands raises questions that go beyond selective interventions and assistance. First and foremost, they oblige the whole global community—and above all the industrialized economies—to switch from half-hearted to consistent measures to reduce emissions. The main reason this necessary political paradigm shift is being shied away from is probably because it would not only have technical implications, but would also call for new forms of ecologically compatible economic activity based on global solidarity. Related to this is the unavoidable, but nonetheless widely avoided question of how painful the changes have to be to capitalist lifestyles and economic systems for the much deeper global wounds perhaps to be healed.

Questions about how we understand migration, citizenship, participation and democracy are no less profound. Years ago, for example, the Kiribati government called for comprehensive migration rights for all its citizens, including free access to employment and education opportunities in the places of their choice. The notion that the global community must also provide separate settlement areas for the inhabitants of islands and areas that have become unliveable is controversial and disturbing even in Kiribati. On the level of principles, it means the right to global citizenship. This is in line with Edgar Morin's visionary conception of the earth as the homeland of all humanity (cf. Morin & Kern 1999; Kramer & Wintersteiner 2021). At the same time, this demand can also be read as meaning that the islands and their inhabitants have already been given up, and all that is left to do is to seek asylum for the climate refugees. For the time being, however, the political debate is about the very definition of "climate refugees"; the people affected do not even fall under the Geneva Refugee Convention and cannot claim a status as refugees.

The existential plight of the atolls in the South Pacific cannot be answered by thinking in terms of North and South. Narrowed down to a single common denominator, what it means is that responsibility for the living conditions on earth cannot be divided on a national level, but is global—in terms not only of the climate, but also of economics, social issues, international law and individual rights. In light of global citizenship, the exercising of that responsibility cannot be controlled from the dominant centers of power; it must involve a fair negotiation process on an equal footing. Talking about the endangered areas is no longer enough, even if it is with the intention of offering what is admittedly impotent help: the discussion has to be with the people living there. This is all the more true when it comes to the powerful discourse on migration as adaptation, various flavours of which also feature in debates on the climate. Local adaptation strategies are often used to avoid facing up to the global implications and to relativize the vulnerabilities, structural problems, hardships and coping skills of people on the ground.

The industrial nations' failure of the century turns out to be the fact that questions of life and death are being decided based on who has the most power, money and potent weapons. This overconfidence rooted in an attitude of paternalism and self-enrichment has failed: today, no-one is safe any more, not even those who still insist that the problem lies elsewhere. Just like in national democracies, global wielders of power must abide by the same rules as everyone: they cannot disregard others. In stable democracies, when it comes to issues that affect the heart of the community and coexistence, such as constitutional law, particularly high majorities are needed to prevent individual lobby groups from making up rules single-handedly. In a global perspective, if the existence of a tiny atoll was threatened by others' behavior, it would have to be given the right of veto, which only the superpowers have in the United Nations. In mature, functioning democracies of the kind that are unfortunately increasingly crumbling under the domination of the media and political lobbies, courts can also stop major decisions if they violate the right of an individual or individual groups.

Migration is not a problem resulting from climate change and other ills in this world; it is an opportunity to gain a new, better understanding of the earth's problems as a global responsibility. It is far from visionary and entirely realistic to say that no-one can escape that responsibility. Everyone must join the discussion, without being allocated any more or fewer rights. This is neither utopian nor an impossibility. Anything else would rather be clinging to the dystopian constitution of our present.

As such, global citizenship is both a definition of our personal right to exist and of political sovereignty that does not depend on the size or power of the political subject. It also means the denationalization of laws, rights and belonging. Wherever people come from and go, they must have a right to exist and participate anywhere in the world. Rather than being a utopian dream, this demand is the "impossible possibility of saying the event" that Derrida calls for (Derrida 2003: 24).

With this issue of the Yearbook on Migration and Society, we would like to help say the event. This extensive subject matter can only be presented rudimentarily in the pages of a book, using individual theoretical approaches and concrete examples. The attempt in this volume to bring climate research from different scientific perspectives into dialogue with critical and reflective migration research also brought together different scientific cultures. As the reviews showed on occasion, those cultures did not always chime fully. In some cases, we found it important here, too, not to demand "adaptation," but to allow different understandings to exist side by side. We hope to contribute to an academic discourse whose inspiration and potential comes from addressing both migration and global society as a means of better understanding complex interrelations. We would like to thank all the authors and reviewers who have contributed to this yearbook:

Helga Kromp-Kolb:
Climate Change and its Challenges

In spite of technological progress and a globalized market, modern societies are not resilient to climate change. An increasing number of people will be forced to migrate due to heat, repeated droughts and floods or rising sea levels. Reducing greenhouse gas emissions to stabilise the climate is an extremely challenging task. The international commitments given at the Conferences of the Parties (COP) of the UN Framework Convention on Climate Change (UNFCCC) are insufficient. The only advance made at COP 2022 was the introduction of a loss and damage fund to support those most affected by extreme events. Since its structures and funding are still uncertain, and the global South is increasingly frustrated by the broken promises of the global North, new mechanisms need to be found to meet the Paris climate goals.

Caroline Schmitt, Robel Afeworki Abay:
The Interplay of the Global Climate Crisis and Forced Migration. From the Imperial Mode of Living to Practices of Conviviality

This article highlights the complex interplay of the global climate crisis and processes of forced migration. In doing so, it rejects simplistic causal explanations and understands global forced migration in the wake of the climate crisis as a multifaceted undertaking that has its origins in the 'imperial mode of living' of the industrialized nations, the externalization of costs associated with it and worsening global inequalities. Based on these findings, this article embarks on a search for convivial practices that envision and seek to implement decolonial and sustainable forms of coexistence in a global society.

Malith De Silva, Nishara Fernando, Pia Hollenbach,
Marco Krüger, Andrea Schmelz, Caroline Schmitt:
Climate Crisis, Global Migration, and Disaster Research.
Social Work as a Bridging Agent

Man-made climate crises have devastating impacts on people's opportunities, capacities and long-term well-being. This article has the following key aims: (a) To provide insights into the nexus of the climate crisis, climate-induced disasters and forced migration, (b) to outline the role of key stakeholders of climate change adaptation and global governance strategies, (c) to showcase the role social work can play as a bridging agent between vulnerable people, disaster response and relief services, and the inter/national governance of disasters and relief and rehabilitation efforts, and (d) to introduce the international and inter-disciplinary network *Connect4Resilience*, formed in 2022 to facilitate, enhance and call attention to gaps in knowledge and practice that are relevant to social impacts of the climate crisis such as forced migration and displacement.

Eva Mach, Mariam Traore Chazalnoël and Dina Ionesco:
Migration in a Changing Climate. What Role Can Migrants'
Remittances Play in Innovative Financing for the
Clean Energy Transition?

The nexus between migration and energy is an emerging field of study in research and policy, but the lack of empirical evidence and academic research on the topic reduces policymakers' ability to develop and implement solutions to observed challenges. With that in mind, our paper seeks to ignite a debate on a specific dimension of migration policy—remittances—and its potential to finance the clean energy transition and help apply a market-based approach that can increase access to clean energy. Remittances have the potential to rewrite the rules of community project financing by putting migrant communities—both sending and receiving—at the center of the energy transition.

Benjamin Schraven:
Der Nexus zwischen Klimawandel und menschlicher Mobilität und
seine besondere Relevanz für urbane Räume

Entgegen alarmistischer Befürchtungen, dass sich schon bald Millionen von „Klimaflüchtlingen" auf den Weg in Richtung Europa machen werden, sprechen die Ergebnisse der Forschungsaktivitäten zum Klima-Mobilitäts-Nexus aus den letzten 20 Jahren für eine deutlich differenziertere Problem-wahrnehmung: So beeinflusst der Klimawandel vor allem Prozesse landes-interner und intraregionaler Migration und Flucht im globalen Süden. Dabei kommt urbanen Gebieten eine besondere Rolle zu: Sie sind die Hauptziele für Migrierende und Geflüchtete, andererseits sind Städte aber auch selbst zunehmend von den negativen Folgen der globalen Erwärmung betroffen. Hinzu kommt, dass Mobilitätsdynamiken zwischen Land und Stadt in vie-lerlei Hinsicht höchst dynamisch sind und wohl auch bleiben werden. Eine entscheidende Grundlage zur besseren politischen Adressierung der daraus resultierenden Herausforderungen ist vor allem ein besseres Verständnis der überaus komplexen Dynamiken menschlicher Mobilität im Kontext des Klimawandels.

Horst Kanzian, Ingrid Huber:
Climate Change Games – Dem Klimawandel spielerisch be- und
entgegnen. Ein methodisch-strategischer Zugang für eine kooperative
Klimabildung

Die Auswirkungen des fortschreitenden anthropogenen Klimawandels sind unüberseh- und spürbar. Für die Gesellschaft erwächst daraus das neue Handlungsfeld, gezielte Maßnahmen zum Klimaschutz und zur Klimawan-delanpassung umzusetzen, um die Folgen des Klimawandels einzudämmen bzw. zu minimieren. In diesem Zusammenhang sind auch Pädagog*innen in Schulen gefragt, die dazu angehalten sind, Klimabildung und -erziehung zu forcieren, damit bei Kindern und Jugendlichen ein klima- und umwelt-bewusstes Denken sowie Handeln resultiert. Dabei stellt sich lehrseits die Frage, mit welchen methodisch-strategischen Zugängen Kompetenzen im Bereich der Klimabildung nachhaltig aufgebaut bzw. erweitert werden kön-nen. Eine Möglichkeit besteht darin, kooperativ und projektorientiert sog. Climate Change Games – also Spiele zum Klimawandel und -schutz – im

Unterricht entwickeln zu lassen, die aus dem Gedankengut der Schüler*innen entspringen. Im entsprechenden Umsetzungssetting, dem kooperativen Lernfeld-Projekt, entstanden auf diese Weise kreative Lernspiele, die die Grundlagen, Ursachen, Zusammenhänge und/oder Auswirkungen des Klimawandels thematisieren und somit besonders bildungs- und handlungswirksam sind. In diesem Kontext sind vielfältige (Lern-) Erfahrungen entstanden, die – neben dem theoretischen Rahmen – in diesem Beitrag erörtert werden.

Brooke Wilmsen, Fazeela Ibrahim:
The Micropolitics of Climate-Related Planned Relocation in the
Maldives. A Case for Multiple Im/mobility Pathways

Climate change adaptation scholars argue that planned relocation should be a last-resort response to climate change. Research, particularly from the perspective of those affected by these interventions, is still in its infancy. To address this gap, we present the findings of a study in 2021 investigating planned relocation on the island of Kolhufushi in the Maldives after the 2004 tsunami. Planned relocation was stalled for almost a decade by complex micropolitics, reaffirming the central role that local knowledge and im/mobility preferences play in producing socially acceptable responses to extreme weather events. Even within one small community, there are multiple im/mobility pathways.

Patrick Sakdapolrak, Harald Sterly:
Building Climate Resilience Through Migration in Thailand

Climate change is increasingly threatening human security, especially among vulnerable populations in the global South, and is influencing migration and mobility patterns. However, the relationship between environmental change and migration is more complex and multilayered than simple representations often suggest. Understanding the degree to which migration can contribute to adaptation requires a translocal and socially differentiated perspective. Taking examples from Thailand, we show the mechanisms driving and conditions surrounding this process.

Literatur/References

Brand, Ulrich/Wissen, Markus (2017): Imperiale Lebensweise. Zur Ausbeutung von Mensch und Natur im globalen Kapitalismus. München: Oekom 2017.

Derrida, Jacques (2003): Eine gewisse unmögliche Möglichkeit, vom Ereignis zu sprechen. Berlin: Merve.

Klein, Sebastian (2022): Wie das Parlament über Fluchtursachen redet. Themenportal Flucht, Migration, Integration: Friedricht-Ebert-Stiftung. https://www.fes.de/themenportal-flucht-migration-integration/artikelseite-flucht-migration-integration/wie-das-parlament-ueber-fluchtursachen-redet vom 31.03.2023.

Klepp, Silja (2013): „Kleine Inselstaaten und die Klimabewegung: Der Fall Kiribati", in: Matthias Dietz/Heiko Garrelts (Hg.), Die internationale Klimabewegung. Ein Handbuch. Wiesbaden: Springer VS, S. 413–428.

Kramer, Gudrun/Wintersteiner, Werner (2021): „Heimatland Erde. Ein Aufruf für planetares Denken und Fühlen, Planen und Handeln.", in: Werner Wintersteiner/Hans Karl Peterlini (Hg.), Die Welt neu denken lernen. Plädoyer für eine planetare Politik. Bielefeld: transcript, S. 205–209.

Lee, Everett S. (1966): "A Theory of Migration", in: Demography, 3(1), S. 47–57, https://doi.org/10.2307/2060063

Lee, Everett S. (1972): „Eine Theorie der Wanderung", in: György Széll (Hg.), Regionale Mobilität. Nymphenburger Verlag 1982, S. 117–129.

Lessenich, Stephan (2016): Neben uns die Sintflut. Die Externalisierungsgesellschaft und ihr Preis. Berlin: Hanser.

Morin, Edgar/Kern, Anne Brigitte (1999): Homeland Earth. New York: Hampton Press.

Morin, Edgar/Kern, Anne Brigitte (1999): Heimatland Erde, Wien: Promedia.

Peterlini, Hans Karl (2023): Learning Diversity. Wiesbaden: Springer VS.

ORF.at (2023): Nehammer: Kürzung von Sozialleistungen „andiskutieren", https://orf.at/stories/3310903/ vom 31.03.2023.

Römhild, Regina/Peterlini, Hans Karl/Danglmaier, Nadja/Donlic, Jasmin (2021): "The border as research space", in: Hans Karl Peterlini/Jasmin Donlic (Hg.), Jahrbuch Migration und Gesellschaft – Yearbook Migration and Society 2020/2021 – „Beyond Borders", Bielefeld: transcript, p. 13–26.

Climate Change and its Challenges

Helga Kromp-Kolb

Climate is essential to human life. Climate determines which plants can grow in a certain region, whether there are lush forests, a diversity of grains, vegetables and fruit, dry savannas, or no plants at all. This in turn determines animal life, which in itself is also dependant on climate. And, of course, human life depends on these resources. Last but not least, vegetation and animal populations in turn influence climate.[1]

When temperatures started systematically dropping at the transition to the last ice age some 100.000 years ago, humans and animals in Europe migrated southward in search of food and warmth. But, one might think, those were primitive tribes, nothing like our highly industrialized and globalized civilisation of today. No need for migration! Were a new ice age to come, should Scandinavia and the Baltic States once more be covered with ice sheets that extend south as far as Denmark, northern Poland and Germany—could we handle this? Wouldn´t all Austrians migrate to the eastern, low lying, ice-free part of the country? Migration would be the only option for a large part of the European population. Migrating might be technically easier than in former times, but would Scandinavians in the millions be welcome in Spain, Italy and Greece? Would Europeans be welcome in Africa and Asia? What used to be an empty world—much space, plenty of resources and few humans—has become a full world—too many people on a limited area of liveable land and with limited resources. This diagnosis by an eminent economist induced him to call for a new type of economy, the present one having been made for an empty world (Daly, 2015).

---

1 This paper partly draws on previous publications in German language by the author.

In the film "The day after tomorrow", a movie that assumes a rapidly growing ice sheet covering half of north America within days, and Americans being evacuated and fleeing to Mexico, Roland Emmerich has the president of the USA saying in an TV-address: "For years we operated under the belief that we could continue consuming our planet's natural resources without consequences. We were wrong. ... Not only Americans, but people all around the globe are now guests in nations we once called the third world. In our time of need they have taken us in and sheltered us and I am deeply grateful for their hospitality." While in the film those forced to migrate essentially caused climate change, in the real world the people most affected have not contributed significantly to climate change and there is no welcoming hospitality when they are forced to migrate.

The world is now experiencing global warming, with a strong likelihood of this getting worse. But within global warming, a collapse of what is commonly called the gulf stream—a section of the global ocean circulation that conveys warm surface waters through the North Atlantic, warming Europe by about 5 °C—could lead to rapidly falling temperatures, increased storm frequency and dryer conditions in Europe within a few years (Thornalley et al., 2018). The weakening or even shutdown of this ocean circulation within this century was a serious consideration in scientific papers some years ago, and an early report to the Pentagon (Schwartz & Randall, 2003) analysed how this would first lead to border disputes, especially over water and farming land, and could end in outright wars. More recent publications do not expect a collapse of the conveyor belt within this century, although a weakening is already observed (IPCC, 2019).

The ficticious scenarios make clear at least two rather obvious things: a) Migration is one form of adaptation to climate change, and in some cases the only option—e. g. in cases of sea level rise, and b) climate change is not just an environmental problem—it is a societal problem with a multitude of interacting consequences.

The Changing Climate

Other than in the ficticious scenarios above, the climate shift experienced in the last decades is one of warming—called by some global heating[2], to avoid the somewhat cosy connotation of the term "warming". While a warming of about 0.17 °C per decade (IPCC, 2021) might seem slow, even negligible to the general public, the scientific evidence is unequivocal that global warming, presently to the extent of about +1.2 °C above pre-industrial levels, has significant consequences. Changing one variable in the climate system has implications for all others, such as moisture, precipitation, pressure and wind systems, and a tendency for extreme events becoming more extreme and often more frequent. In fact, the report by the Intergovernmental Panel on Climate Change (IPCC, 2018) that was produced to clarify whether a 1.5 °C limit to warming would provide significant advantages over the 2 °C goal of the Paris agreement, concluded that every tenth of a degree of warming matters. For example, at +1.5 °C, 700 million people would be affected by extreme heat waves at least once every 20 years; at +2 °C, 2 billion would be affected. At +1.5 °C, about 11% of the land area would be affected by flooding along rivers, at +2 °C it would be 21%; the North Pole would become ice-free in 40 years at the end of summer in one case, in 3 to 5 years in the other. Hence, the difference between 1.5 °C and 2 °C is huge in terms of effects. Many climate elements, as well as parts of the biosphere, respond at even smaller temperature increases than scientists previously expected (IPCC, 2023a, 2023b). Since the reactions are typically exponential rather than linear, even small temperature differences or minor misjudgements can have far-reaching consequences.

Some scientific publications (Kemp et al., 2022; Lenton et al., 2019; Ripple et al., 2023; Steffen et al., 2018) indicate that stabilization of the climate system may not be possible at warming levels above 2 °C. A dynamic of constant warming, "hothouse earth", could emerge because tipping points of the climate system are exceeded, leading to self-reinforcement of warming. Mankind would be powerless against it and the end of our civilization would be the consequence. "Hothouse earth" is not an expected development based

---

2 E.g. Richard Betts, UK Met Office, and Hans Joachim Schellnhuber, PIK, as quoted in https://www.theguardian.com/environment/2018/dec/13/global-heating-more-accurate-to-describe-risks-to-planet-says-key-scientist

on established knowledge, but it is considered too risky to try ("too risky to bet against").

Current policy indicates a temperature increase of 2.8 °C by the end of the century. Implementing current national pledges will only reduce temperature rise to 2.4 °C for conditional pledges or 2.6 °C for unconditional pledges. However, countries are not currently on the pledged emissions pathway (UNEP, 2022). +1.5 °C is likely to be permanently exceeded by the early 2030s. This means that drastic greenhouse gas emission reductions are needed within this decade to avoid the risk of "hothouse earth".

The fact that the 27th Conference of the Parties to the United Nations Framework Convention on Climate Change (COP27) did not make any progress in this respect is tragic in view of the time pressure: Neither did the parties to the UN Framework convention of climate change (UNFCCC) commit themselves to significantly improving their reduction targets, nor was the phase-out of coal made more concrete. On the contrary, some Glasgow formulations were even weakened (Ramachandran, 2022): Instead of a 45% reduction in emissions by 2030 compared to 2010, only a 43% reduction compared to 2019 is required. Given the increase in emissions between 2010 and 2019, this is a significant step backwards. The timeline for achieving net zero is missing altogether.

Unfortunately, it's not about just one lost year. The success of international climate conferences depends on the host country working hard in the run-up to the conference. The next COP will be held in Dubai. As one of the oil-richest countries in the world, Dubai sees renewable energy as a supplement to, not a replacement for, fossil fuels. But not phasing out fossil fuels makes it impossible to meet the 1.5 °C target. For the COP in 2024, the Czech Republic, Bulgaria and Australia are in discussion; none of them is known to have particularly ambitious national climate goals. Real progress brought by the COPs in the next two years would therefore be a surprise.

Loss and Damage

The COP27 did, however, make progress in one important aspect, even though it is of a more symbolic nature. Following the devastating floods in Pakistan in 2022 which affected 33 million people, killed over 1500 people and caused an estimated US$30 billion in damage (Gerhardt, 2022), Pakistan has pushed to put the issue of loss and damage on the agenda of COP27, two years earlier than scheduled. The issue had come up at climate conferences since 1991, when it was raised by the small island nation of Vanuatu.

There is no doubt that the industrialized nations have caused a substantial part of man-made climate change, while the developing countries[3] are suffering the most. Regarding a quantification of the share of climate change in damages caused by extreme events, science has made great progress in recent years in an exemplary international and interdisciplinary collaboration termed "attribution science" (van Oldenborgh et al., 2021). One aspect of this new methodology is simulating the actual weather situation in a world that is 1.2 °C cooler, and looking at the differences to calculations based on the current situation. Furthermore, statistical analyses are performed using observed time series. The methodology allows quantifications in many cases, but large uncertainties remain depending on the event considered. Other changes, such as altered building development, or extent of precautions against extreme events must also be taken into account, if the extent of damage is addressed. While there still are fundamental problems in quantifying loss and damage realistically, the quality of the assessments has reached such a level that attribution studies are already finding their way into legal disputes.

The floods in Pakistan, for example, were caused by unusually heavy monsoon rains and melting glaciers due to a severe heat wave in the preceding months, both probably exacerbated by climate change. However, the amounts of monsoon precipitation, which vary widely from year to year, are still poorly captured by climate models, so that model-based confirmation of the rather high contribution of climate change inferred from observed time series is only tentative. Undoubtedly, however, according to the scientists of the world weather attribution project, the proximity of settlements, infrastructure and agricultural land to the floodplains, inadequate infrastructure, limited ex ante risk mitigation capacity, an outdated river management system, vulnerability due to high poverty rates and socioeconomic factors, and ongoing political and economic instability, all contributed to the magni-

---

3 The terms developing countries and Third World have largely been replaced in migration discourse by the term Global South, distinguished from the Global North. These terms are not geographical but a description of global inequality. If this article also refers to developing countries, it is because policy measures and funds are named this way.

tude of the disaster. Hence, it is difficult to put a number on the damage or the loss due to climate change in this case. (Otto et al., 2022)

Thus, while there is little question about the fundamental legitimacy of developing countries' demands for compensation for loss and damage, industrialized nations resist a formal recognition of an obligation to pay. Since the damage is becoming greater and more diverse as climate change progresses, and an increasing number of areas is affected, the industrialized countries also fear that admitting a payment obligation would open up a bottomless pit.

Due to massive pressure from the Alliance of Small Island States (AOSIS), supported by the G77, it was finally agreed to create a fund from which aid payments would be made, but not by whom and how it would be filled[4]. The terms of disbursement also remained open. In view of the hesitancy with which the Green Climate Fund (GCF), which was already agreed in Paris, is being stocked and the fact that the volume falls well short of the original pledge[5], it is to be feared that the new fund will only divert further resources from the GCF. The number of relevant funds is growing: In addition to the Green Climate Fund and now the Loss and Damage Fund, the Least Developed Countries Fund, the Special Climate Change Fund, the Adaptation Fund and the Global Environment Facility are waiting to be filled to the agreed extent.

In 2015, the industrialized nations' generous funding commitments to the Green Climate Fund were a condition of the developing countries' agreement to the Paris Agreement. Not surprisingly, developing countries are assessing their levers to achieve real support, and thinking aloud about a global creditor strike: breach of promise versus breach of promise. Developing countries' refusal to make interest payments on their debts could create movement in the political arena via the financial sector. As US climate activist Bill McKibben notes: "Justice makes progress only through politics. Balancing the world's wealth even a little is the most difficult of all political tasks. But our chances for a liveable world may depend on it". (McKibben, 2022)

---

4 https://unfccc.int/sites/default/files/resource/TC1%20Paper%203%20Workplan%2029%20March%20rev3.pdf?download

5 https://www.greenclimate.fund/about/resource-mobilisation/gcf-1

Climate Change Is not Just an Environmental Problem

While it has been clear from the outset that climate change is not just an issue of rising temperatures and enhanced extreme events, but has far reaching societal, economic, and political implications, this does not seem to have been understood by the general public and possibly not sufficiently by politicians. The interaction of the natural environment with economic, societal and political activities makes climate change a societal problem. In a recent article some of these interactions and their feedbacks were described in a more systemic way, using a simplified causal loop diagram (Kemp et al., 2022) to show how risk cascades could unfold: Global warming causes sea level rise and extreme weather events that both can lead to displacements and thus to international and local conflicts. These also become more likely as economic inequality increases, which again can be the result of global warming and e. g. extreme heat waves. Resource shortages, such as water, food and fuel can be intensified by sea level rise and extreme weather events, but also as a consequence of political instability and state fragility resulting from displacements and conflicts. All these factors increase mortality. The positive feedbacks in this system—e. g. displacements causing political instability and state fragility undermining law and order and the ability of states to feed their population, which in turn increased migration—exacerbate the problems.

What people suffer from most is generally not the change in climate in itself, but its immediate consequences, such as drought and famine, or indirect consequences such as civil war. In addition to the debt trap in which developing countries find themselves, a climate trap has developed, where modest prosperity is lost again with the next extreme weather event (McKibben, 2022). Recovery from devastating events such as hurricanes or floods like those in Pakistan can take years.

Needless to say, within every country it is the poor that suffer most, generally being placed in more exposed locations (flood plains, densely populated cities) and having the least means to cope with gradual changes and disaster (Rigaud et al., 2018). On the other hand, there is plenty of experience that often these people are better equipped to meet smaller scale disruptions by long tested experience of shortages of all sorts and high adaptability than people unused to coping with disruptions and highly dependent on technical support in their daily lives—as is true for many in industrialized countries.

Not only adaptation or its limits make climate change more than an environmental problem, mitigation also is predominantly a societal problem. It is not—as often framed—a purely technological problem.

Mitigation of GHG Emissions

To stay within the 1.5 °C limit with 50% probability, global GHG emissions must be reduced to 50% by 2030, and net zero must be achieved by 2050, at which point the GHG budget will be exhausted (WMO, 2022). The global budget can be calculated for individual countries by population. For Austria (CCCA et al., 2022), e.g., this results in a budget of 430 Mt CO_2 from the beginning of 2022. With annual emissions of about 70 Mt CO_2 per year, the budget would be exhausted in 6 years, i.e. at the end of 2028, without effective mitigation measures. If 50% probability of complying with the Paris Agreement is not deemed enough—at 66% the still permissible emission for Austria drops to 240 Mt CO_2. Staying within this budget requires a reduction of half of the emissions about every 2–3 years. The situation is similar for other European countries. It is obvious that this is an almost unmanageable challenge.

These budget considerations show that there is no time to wait for new technologies to emerge: Emission reductions to 50% within less than ten years can only be achieved with existing technologies such as renewable energies and higher efficiency and must essentially rely on existing infrastructure. The hydrogen economy or nuclear developments such as small modular nuclear reactors (SMR) or fusion energy—even if their sustainability were not questionable and they were considered highly desirable—would not penetrate the market in time. Hydrogen will play a role in some niches, such as powering energy intensive machines, but it will not be a panacea for all energy problems. In addition to renewable energy large contributions through increased efficiency and sufficiency will be needed.

Chancellor Angela Merkel noted in 2021, when visiting the Ahrtal after it was devastated by a deathly flood "We need a full transformation of our economy, of our way of doing business."[6] The encouraging aspect is that the

---

6 https://www.wiwo.de/politik/deutschland/merkel-in-den-usa-kampf-gegen-klimawandel
-erfordert-eine-volltransformation-der-art-des-wirtschaftens/27426772.html

necessary changes can lead to a more equitable and just world with higher quality of life, albeit lower standards of living as measured by goods and services.

The energy sector was already addressed—a decentralised system based on renewable energy would not only stop money drain from communities and states, but also dramatically change the geopolitical situation, possibly bringing peace to regions that have been in turmoil over fossil resources for decades. An industry producing more durable, high quality products that can be repaired and recycled in a circular economy, with possession in many cases less attractive than rental (e.g. drills, cars) would mean enormous savings in resources, including energy. Though the individual product might have a higher price, such a system could bring financial relief to low income families.(Kirchengast et al., 2019)

This is not the place to enlarge upon similar schemes for mobility systems that are conductive to improved health and safety, agriculture that is resilient and produces healthy soils and food, a health system that focusses on prevention and health rather than on costly remedies shifting money from the state to the pharmaceutical industry, an educational system fostering creativity, self-efficacy, confidence and cooperation in the young, a financial system that serves the real economy, possibly based on a biotope of currencies, and democracies reverting to their original intent, fostering participation and ethics of responsibility.

Fundamentally, all these changes are directed towards two agendas that are also at the root of the UN 2030 Agenda and the Sustainable Development Goals (SDGs): Ensuring or enabling a "good life for all" (human well-being) while respecting ecological limits. The challenge is to pursue both synergistically and not play them off against each other. In past decades, a common idea based on the environmental Kuznet´s curve as interpreted by (Grossman & Krueger, 1991), was that a society must first become more prosperous to then take care of the environment. This has proven to be a fallacy, because as prosperity has increased, so has resource use, and none of the nations that have achieved the desired prosperity—as measured, for example, by the "human development index," HDI,—have reduced their ecological footprint to the required level (Kromp-Kolb & Formayer, 2018). This is not proof that it cannot be done, it just has not been seriously attempted to date. Thus, the task of the industrialized nations is to reduce the ecological footprint back to a sustainable level and at the same time improve the quality of life of its citizens to make the transformation attractive. The challenge for the developing countries is to create at least a minimum of quality of life for all their citizens without increasing the ecological footprint significantly.

These are fundamental changes, but necessary, as nature is not an inexhaustible reservoir of resources that humans can use at will, but a complex system of which humans are a part. Nature is the basis of human life—we must therefore learn to want only what we can achieve within the limits set by nature. For humanity as a whole, but especially for people in industrialized countries, this means learning to be satisfied with less, i.e. to accept a sufficiency principle. Some of the things we thought we were entitled to will not be attainable—such as the German dream of a private home in the countryside for everyone, or the annual flight to some far away vacation paradise, meat three times a day or even every fruit in every season. Although this may sound like renunciation and doing without, in essence it is a matter of change from a but recently acquired culture of plenty and waste and a matter of change of habits.

A Path Forward?

There is no doubt that the framework conditions for the COP27 were not favourable with the energy and food crisis as a result of the Ukraine war that preoccupied especially Europe, the USA and Russia. Sustainability is intimately tied to peace—not only in Europe, but worldwide. In the long run, peace and sustainability are inseparable. Therefore, efforts to achieve peace are a step towards resolving the climate issue that cannot be overrated. Peace is important and it is urgent!

On the practical level of international climate negotiations, one must seriously ask whether it is still justifiable to tie the development of climate policy to the COPs, indeed whether the COPs themselves still make sense. It seems very questionable whether *the great leap forward*, that is now asked for (Dixson-Declève et al., 2021) with five major turnarounds (poverty, inequality, empowerment, food, and energy, as well as a major restructuring of the economic system) can be achieved collectively, or whether it is up to individual countries to demonstrate, at least selectively, that this leap can be made without social disruption and economic catastrophe.

Several options are being discussed (see e.g. McKibben, 2022), apart from continuing as before, with even more concerted effort to convince the nations of the world that common long-term goals are more important than national short-term successes. Some form of coalition of the willing to make real progress on emissions reductions within this group, even if not all nations participate, might bring the issue forward; the Beyond Coal and Gas Alliance is a step in that direction. Bilateral agreements, such as between the U.S. and China, could be systematically advanced and play a more important role. Teaming between individual or groups of industrialized and developing countries to transfer technology and funds to developing countries to enable development without depleting their greenhouse gas budgets, and, in return, entitling the industrialized nations to use the unspent part of the budget of the respective partners might enable a realistically achievable emission reduction path for industrialized countries. Helping developing countries become more attractive for private investments could funnel money in the Global North seeking investment opportunities, such as pension funds, to the Global South to develop renewable energy there. Cushioning the risks of such investments through international development banks or the World Bank could go some way to achieving this. The Bridgetown Agenda of the Prime Minister of Barbados would be an example.

None of these options may be convincing, but until better ones are found, they should be pursued in parallel. Otherwise, the only option left is to abandon the idea of meeting the 1.5 °C target, accepting the ethically unacceptable risk of ending up in a hothouse earth state. But nobody can seriously want that. In Greta Thunberg's words: It is a matter of making the necessary possible!

References

CCCA, Steininger, K./Schinko, T./Rieder, H./Kromp-Kolb, H./Kienberger, S./.../Lambert, S. (2022): 1,5 °C: Wieviel Treibhausgase dürfen wir noch emittieren? Hintergrundpapier zu globalen und nationalen Treibhausgasbudgets. 27. Retrieved from https://ccca.ac.at/thg-budget

Daly, H. (2015): Economics for a full world. Retrieved from https://greattransition.org/images/Daly-Economics-Full-World.pdf

Dixson-Declève, S./Gaffney, O./Ghosh, J./Randers, J./Rockström, J./Stoknes, P. E. (2021): Earth for all. A survival guide for humanity. Report to the Club of Rome: oekom Verlag.

Gerhardt, T. (2022, November 23). "In a Historic Move, Frontline Communities Will Be Compensated for Climate Crisis Impacts", in: The Nation. Retrieved from https://www.thenation.com/article/environment/cop27-loss-damage-compensation/

Grossman, G./Krueger, A. (1991): Environmental Impacts of a North American Free Trade Agreement. Retrieved from https://EconPapers.repec.org/RePEc:fth:priwpu:158

IPCC (2018): Global Warming of 1.5°C. An IPCC Special Report on the impacts of global warming of 1.5°C above pre-industrial levels and related global greenhouse gas emission pathways, in the context of strengthening the global response to the threat of climate change, sustainable development, and efforts to eradicate poverty, ed. by V. Masson-Delmotte/P. Zhai/H.-O. Pörtner/D. Roberts/J. Skea/P.R. Shukla/A. Pirani/W. Moufouma-Okia/C. Péan/R. Pidcock/S. Connors/J.B.R. Matthews/Y. Chen/X. Zhou/M.I. Gomis/E. Lonnoy/T. Maycock/M. Tignor/T. Waterfield.

IPCC (2019): IPCC Special Report on the Ocean and Cryosphere in a Changing Climate, Cambridge, UK/New York, NY, USA: Cambridge University Press.

IPCC (2021): Climate Change 2021: The Physical Science Basis. Contribution of Working Group I to the Sixth Assessment Report of the Intergovernmental Panel on Climate Change, ed. by V. Masson-Delmotte/P. Zhai/S. L. Pirani/C. P. Connors/S. N. Berger/Y. Caud/L. Chen/M. I. Goldfarb/M. Gomis/K. Huang/E. Leitzell/J. B. R. Lonnoy/T. K. Matthews/T. Maycock/O. Waterfield/R. Y. Yelekçi/B. E. Zhou, Cambridge University Press.

IPCC (2023a): Synthesis Report of the IPCC Sixth Asssessment Report (AR6). Longer Report.

IPCC (2023b): Synthesis Report of the IPCC Sixth Asssessment Report (AR6). Summary for Policymakers.

Kemp, L./Xu, C./Depledge, J./Ebi, K. L./Gibbins, G./Kohler, T. A./.../Lenton, T. M. (2022): "Climate Endgame: Exploring catastrophic climate change scenarios", in: Proceedings of the National Academy of Sciences, 119(34), e2108146119. https://doi.org/10.1073/pnas.2108146119

Kirchengast, G./Kromp-Kolb, H./Steininger, K./Stagl, S./Kirchner, M./ Ambach, C./.../Strunk, B. (2019): Referenzplan als Grundlage für einen wissenschaftlich fundierten und mit den Pariser Klimazielen in Einklang stehenden Nationalen Energie- und Klimaplan für Österreich (Ref-NEKP). Retrieved from https://ccca.ac.at/wissenstransfer/uninetz-sdg-13/referenz-nationaler-klima-und-energieplan-ref-nekp

Kromp-Kolb, H./Formayer, H. (2018): 2 Grad. Warum wir uns für die Rettung der Welt erwärmen sollten, Wien/Graz: Molden.

Lenton, T. M./Rockström, J./Gaffney, O./Rahmstorf, S./Richardson, K./ Steffen, W./Schellnhuber, H. J. (2019): Climate tipping points — too risky to bet against, in: Nature, 575 (28 November 2019), 592.

McKibben, B. (2022, November 19). "How to Pay for Climate Justice When Polluters Have All the Money. The COP27 climate conference, in Egypt, was in large part a global search for cash." Daily Comment, in: The New Yorker. Retrieved from https://www.newyorker.com/news/daily-comment/how-to-pay-for-climate-justice-when-polluters-have-all-the-money

Otto, F. E. L./Zachariah, M./Saeed, F./Siddiqi, A./Shahzad, K./Mushtaq, H./.../Clarke, B. (2022). Climate change likely increased extreme monsoon rainfall, flooding highly vulnerable communities in Pakistan. Retrieved from https://www.worldweatherattribution.org/wp-content/uploads/Pakistan-floods-scientific-report.pdf

Ramachandran, R. (2022). COP27 fails to improve on COP26 but loss and damage fund the saving grace, in: Frontline. India's National Magazine. Retrieved from https://frontline.thehindu.com/environment/cop27-fails-to-improve-on-cop26-but-loss-and-damage-fund-the-saving-grace/article66182841.ece

Rigaud, K. K./de Sherbinin, A./Jones, B./Bergmann, J./Clement, V./Ober, K./.../Midgley, A. (2018): Groundswell: Preparing for internal climate migration, Washington DC: World Bank.

Ripple, W. J./Wolf, C./Lenton, T. M./Gregg, J. W./Natali, S. M./Duffy, P. B./.../ Schellnhuber, H. J. (2023): "Many risky feedback loops amplify the need for climate action", in: One Earth, 6(2), p. 86–91. https://doi.org/10.1016/ j.oneear.2023.01.004

Schwartz, P./Randall, D. (2003): An Abrupt Climate Change Scenario and Its Implications for United States National Security. Retrieved from Washington: http://stephenschneider.stanford.edu/Publications/PDF_Papers/ SchwartzRandall2004.pdf, http://purl.access.gpo.gov/GPO/LPS69716

Steffen, W./Rockstrom, J./Richardson, K./Lenton, T. M./Folke, C./Liverman, D./.../Schellnhuber, H. J. (2018). "Trajectories of the Earth System in the Anthropocene", in: Proc Natl Acad Sci USA, 115(33), 8252-8259. https://doi.org/ 10.1073/pnas.1810141115

Thornalley, D. J. R./Oppo, D. W./Ortega, P./Robson, J. I./Brierley, C. M./Davis, R.,/.../Keigwin, L. D. (2018): "Anomalously weak Labrador Sea convection and Atlantic overturning during the past 150 years", in: Nature, 556(7700), 227-230. https://doi.org/10.1038/s41586-018-0007-4

UNEP (2022): Emission Gap Report 2022: The closing Window—Climate crisis calls for rapid transformation of societies, Nairobi: UNEP.

van Oldenborgh, G. J./van der Wiel, K./Kew, S./Sjoukje, P./Otto, F./Vautard, R./.../van Aalst, M. (2021): Pathways and Pitfalls in extreme event attribution. Retrieved from https://www.worldweatherattribution.org/ pathways-and-pitfalls-in-extreme-event-attribution/

WMO (2022): (Provisional) WMO Statement on the state of the Global Climate in 2022. Geneva.

The Interplay of the Global Climate Crisis and Forced Migration
From the Imperial Mode of Living to Practices of Conviviality

Caroline Schmitt, Robel Afeworki Abay

The global climate crisis is not only an ecological disaster, but must be analysed as a multiple catastrophic phenomenon representing the intersection of ecological, social, economic and existential crises. This complex aspect has for instance been increasingly discussed in the context of growing forced migration movements. According to different forecasts, by 2050 the climate crisis could lead to more than 200 million people around the world fleeing their places of residence and countries (e.g. Statista 2022). In the 2022 report by the International Panel on Climate Change (IPCC), it is assumed that each degree of temperature increase also increases the global risks of involuntary migration by 50% of the previous value (quoted by Hillmann 2022: 6). However, caution is needed with all of these figures since it is often not clear how the data are collected (ibid.). While figures certainly raise awareness of the threats posed by the climate crisis, they do not provide detailed information about its structural causes and the forced migration movements associated with them.

Bearing this in mind, the aim of this article is to highlight the complex interplay of the global climate crisis and processes of forced migration. In doing so, it rejects simplistic causal explanations and understands global forced migration in the wake of the climate crisis as a multifaceted phenomenon originating in the 'imperial mode of living' adopted by industrialized nations, the externalization of the costs associated with it and how this amplified the global inequalities of many marginalized communities, especially in the Global South. As Carsten Felgentreff (2015) accurately points out, the complex debate on 'climate refugees' must not lead us to trivialize problematic societal situations and blame the changing climate alone for the displacement and forced migration of people from the Global South (ibid: 141). Rather, it is important to take the climate crisis as one of several starting points to examine the socially and politically manufactured causes of forced migration from the perspective of global inequality.

For this reason, Ulrich Brand and Markus Wissen's (2017, 2022) concept of the 'imperial mode of living' makes a suitable starting point for a critical examination of contemporary forms of power and dominance by the Global North. Brand and Wissen (2017) argue that the capitalist social order exploits the socio-ecological resources in countries of the Global South in favor of consumption and economic growth in capitalist centers. This makes it impossible, they assert, for everyone in the world to enjoy a 'good life' and a fair distribution of resources, a fact that has often been ignored by the discourses, institutions and practices of the Global North. Hence, imperialism functions as a constitutive basis of global capitalism, rendering the existing asymmetrical power relations between the Global North and Global South invisible. Working on this basis, this article[1] explores the multiple and shifting ways in which the global climate crisis intersects with forced migration. Based on these reflections, it pleads for convivial practices that seek to implement decolonial, sustainable structures of coexistence in our global society.

On the Interconnectedness of the Global Climate Crisis and Forced Migration

The fact that the global climate crisis and forced migration processes are interconnected in many ways should not be understood either as natural or as unalterable. The concept of the 'imperial mode of living' states that global inequalities, the climate crisis, wars and poverty, and intra-societal and global processes of division threaten livelihoods around the world. However, state crisis policies and public debates are strongly oriented toward supporting

---

1   Please note that this article contains some passages from a paper we previously published in German (Afeworki Abay/Schmitt 2022), which we have further refined.

the dominant economic and social model (Brand/Wissen 2022). While some people have access to material prosperity, security and social services, the livelihoods of marginalized groups of people and the resources of the planet are being destroyed. Brand and Wissen's (ibid.) analysis is designed to show the necessity of looking for alternatives and countering the imperial model with the idea of a solidarity-based life. The growing climate crisis, however, highlights the urgency of not just thinking about sustainable and future-oriented forms of economic activity and coexistence, but also implementing them. Adhering to the capitalist logic of constant growth appears to run the risk of missing the 1.5-degree target agreed in the Paris Climate Agreement. In order to achieve this goal, global greenhouse gas emissions have to be reduced quickly, while environmentally harmful production methods and lifestyles have to be replaced by sustainable ones.

Many scholars have already pointed out that global inequality is a fundamental problem, as it is primarily the industrialized nations and wealthy sections of the world's population that are responsible for the majority of human-made CO_2 emissions. At the same time, marginalized groups of people, people affected by poverty and racialized people are already suffering particularly from the effects of the climate crisis. Ulrike Brizay (2012) points out that it is mostly people in countries of the Global South who are increasingly being displaced from their familiar living environment by extreme weather events as a result of global warming. Samia Aden and Samira Aden (2021) argue on the basis of their field research in Somalia that nomadic people are being forced to abandon their nomadic way of life due to climate-related droughts. They have been scattered throughout the country as internally displaced persons, and are now dependent on humanitarian aid.

Among others, Sophia Wirsching (2015) draws attention to a central point: when the climate crisis interacts with other problematic situations to trigger forced migration processes, millions of people are not able to migrate and flee from places, although they are particularly exposed to environmental crises there. Their immobilization due to a lack of resources to spatially escape the negative effects of the global climate crisis is a point that needs further debate. It shows that responsible parties in industrialized nations, especially, need to fundamentally address and challenge the existing 'imperial mode of living' of the Global North. At the same time, climate-induced migration is no longer an issue affecting the Global South alone, as shown by climate-related natural disasters such as the floods in the Ahr Valley in Germany in July 2021 (Liedholz 2021a). One difference between marginalized regions in the Global South and capitalist centers, however, is that the latter can afford to ignore climate and environmental problems for a relatively long time thanks to their social security systems. They have the resources to adapt, such as by strengthening dikes, or to pay compensation (Hillmann 2022: 15). These unequal opportunities to respond to climate and environmental crises demonstrate the importance of addressing global inequalities when dealing with the climate crisis and, in doing so, translating principles of equity and global responsibility into policy action. The climate crisis, it can be argued, is being produced by a wealthy elite and borne on the shoulders of marginalized people—who, in the worst case, are losing their lives or their living environment and livelihoods.

Gayatri Spivak (2007) already pointed out this connection almost two decades ago. Even then, she noted that the environmentally destructive production and consumption practices of the Global North play a role in consolidating the post- and neocolonial order of capitalist relations of exploitation and inequality in the Global South. For example, a Euro-American child consumes 183 times as many resources as a child from the so-called 'Third World' (ibid: 149). Similarly, presenting his concept of Slow Violence, Rob Nixon (2011) describes these global inequalities as fatal to more socially just and ecological world relations. Jason Hickel (2020: 403) criticizes these unequal relations as ecological imperialism: "Should post-colonial states be held responsible for territorial emissions generated by colonial governments? Or should responsibility for those emissions be allocated at least in part to the relevant colonial power, on the grounds that they were the primary beneficiaries of the underlying industrial processes?"

Many scholars posit that the socio-ecological, political and economic consequences of the climate crisis are further cementing not only the socially and economically unequal structures that exist in the Global South, but also the post- and neocolonial entanglement between the Global North and South (among others: Mayblin 2017; Castro Varela 2018; Achiume 2019). This aggravation is due to various factors, such as a lack of social protection systems, or insufficient access to them by subaltern groups (Brand/Wissen 2017). Lack of social protection leads to increasingly complex hardship against the backdrop of the dramatic impacts of the climate crisis—which include droughts, floods, storms, famines and damage to infrastructure (Weerasinghe 2018): People are dying; poverty, conflicts and forced migration are on the rise and are mutually dependent. In July 2021, for example, the World Meteorological Organization (WMO 2021), a specialized agency of the United Nations, noted that between the years 1970 and 2019, more than one million people died from droughts (650,000 deaths), storms (577,232 deaths), floods (58,700 deaths) and extreme temperatures (55,736 deaths). Nixon (2011) theorized that the climate crisis, habitat and biodiversity destruction, livelihood loss and forced migration movements are closely intertwined. Despite these findings, the climate crisis and global inequalities have not yet been enshrined in the 1951 Geneva Convention Relating to the Status of Refugees as reasons for forced migration and asylum.

Ecosocial Real Utopias

The authors of this article position themselves in the field of international, postcolonial, solidarity-based social work. Social work has a mandate to create inclusion, social justice, equality, solidarity and participation. It must always get involved when social protection becomes fragile, when people are pushed to the margins of society and when mounting crises and disasters particularly affect marginalized groups of people—as is the case in the climate crisis (Aden/Aden 2021; Kleibl/Lutz/Noyoo 2020; Khoo/Kleibl 2020). In this context, postcolonially informed perspectives are of great importance in revealing the central inequality-generating structures of world society and the resulting manifold, complex entanglements between that inequality and social discrimination—and in working on these issues by means of critical/reflexive research and practice (Castro Varela/Mohamed 2021; Afeworki Abay/Wechuli 2022). The authors agree with Yannick Liedholz (2021b), among others, that social work must take a position in the debates about whether and how Europe and the industrialized nations have a duty to offer protection to people fleeing their countries due to climate change and related problems.

We see a need to revise the legally recognized reasons for forced migration, and consider a fundamental examination of ecosocial initiatives to be central—against the background of strengthening such approaches and making known their relevance to society as a whole. By ecosocial initiatives we mean those that oppose the mechanism of dividing the world into 'us' and 'them' (Anderson 2013; Or 2022)—and thus work on the causes of the climate crisis and the 'imperial mode of living' and propose counter-concepts. Such mechanisms dichotomizing the global society are vividly described by Stephan Lessenich (2020) in his work on the externalization of societies. Using the term 'externalization,' Lessenich emphasizes how processes of separation maintain capitalist societies' mode of production and way of life, where possible leaving the collateral damage and consequential costs of capitalist exploitation in external economic and social spaces, or transferring them there (ibid.). This includes CO2 emissions, waste and cheap labor (Peterlini 2023).

This failure to take responsibility for the destruction of a more inclusive, just global togetherness, and of our ecological foundations, is increasingly being criticized not just by ecosocial initiatives but also by scientific associations. In real laboratories, manifestos and concrete practices in the city and in the countryside, community-based concepts, post-growth approaches, and indigenous philosophies are being developed or rediscovered that reach far beyond questions of global forced migration: they deal fundamentally and sustainably with our togetherness in the world. Despite their diversity, these concepts focus on the unifying potential of community and aim to become active in the here and now. One concept that can bracket the many approaches is conviviality.

The Concept of Conviviality

The concept of conviviality is significantly influenced by Ivan Illich (1973). Even in the 1970s, Illich (1973) already saw this term as a critique of limitless, industrial growth and mass production that exploits people's capacities and has the potential to destroy communities. By 'convivial' he meant a society in which technologies serve individuals and not managers and in which actors act responsibly in the world. Following Illich's concept of conviviality, a small group of initiators was formed at a colloquium in Japan in 2010 (first and foremost: Alain Caillé, Marc Humbert, Serge Latouche and Patrick Viveret). The group wanted to concretize the concept of conviviality against the backdrop of global crises. Finally, in 2011, sociologist Alain Caillé formulated and published a preliminary version of the convivialist manifesto, which was then intensively discussed and revised by a larger group of around 40 people before being published in 2013 (Adloff 2021: 3). The Convivialist Manifesto and the subsequent Second Manifesto develop ideas for creating a socially just, ecologically and politically responsible form of human coexistence, going beyond growth ideologies and neoliberalism (Adloff/Leggewie 2014; Die konvivialistische Internationale 2020). The manifestos call for a search for new forms of shared inhabitation of the world. The authors argue in favor of degrowth, treating the planet in a manner that conserves its resources, de-marketization and the assumption of ecological responsibility.

The word *convivialité* is quite common in French and 'conviviality' has also become established in English in this meaning. Recently, it has been used in discussions about living together in migration societies (Adloff/Heins 2015: 9). While the term 'conviviality' denotes a practice of living together, 'convivialism' is about systematizing a social and political perspective on a theoretical level (ibid.: 10). Fundamentally, the practice of conviviality is about decoupling ideas of a good life from the capitalist growth paradigm and linking science, practical convivial experiments and civil society actors in the search for solidary, just, sustainable forms of being together in the world (ibid: 11).

In our view, the potential of convivial perspectives lies in bringing together different discourses around marginalization and discrimination, examining how they are connected through an intersectional lens and combining them to study how a good life can be possible for everyone. In light of concerns about how to respond to the climate crisis, a move away from neoliberal principles and toward ecological stewardship can be seen as a move towards more justice. This highlights that growth-oriented lifestyles—for example, involving the overuse of water resources or extensive deforestation—have led to people being exposed to water scarcity, drought or landslides, being deprived of their livelihoods and having to leave their living environment.

The concept of conviviality, by contrast, directs our attention to contexts in which people live and work together in an ecosocial, sustainable way. Such forms of togetherness can already be found in cities and in the countryside. They are seen in contexts such as shared green spaces, solidarity-based farming concepts or sustainable housing projects. This sets a task for research and practice: both the potentials and limitations of such practices need to be further explored and sustainable projects need to be institutionalized and supported (in detail see the works of Elsen, e.g. Elsen 2018). This task is, in our view, an interdisciplinary and interprofessional as well as a political task.

Conclusion

This contribution has shown that the global climate crisis is interlinked with forced migration processes; how the major problems of our time are part of the 'imperial mode of living' and post- and neocolonial structures of capitalist exploitation and global inequality. The climate crisis and related problems such as poverty, natural disasters and global forced migration call for a fundamental shift towards sustainable and convivial modes of living. While international and national policies do not tend to show any signs of a consistent change of direction, ecosocial movements and laboratories for convivial transformation are emerging at the local level and in associations of practitioners and scientists. The ideas they generate need to be shifted from the margins to the center of the debates. Social research can contribute to this by drawing attention to visionary and decolonial practices by integrating them into teaching as well as advocating for social policies on climate crisis and forced migration that are critical of geopolitical power and work towards inclusion.

Moreover, theoretical reflection reveals a fundamental tension between the rarely questioned principle of growth in global capitalism, on the one hand, and ecosocial real utopias in a post-capitalist world, on the other. In this chapter, we plead for that tension to be used as a chance to examine the colonial continuity of Western domination, hegemonic structures of oppression and the privileged position of an elite minority, in order to come ever closer to the goal of ecosocial coexistence and whole-planet thinking.

References

Achiume, Tendayi E. (2019): "Migration as Decolonization", in: Stanford Law Review, 1509/71, pp. 1509–1574.

Aden, Samia/Aden, Samira (2021): "Klimawandel und Fluchtmigration.", in: Julia Devlin/Tanja Evers/Simon Goebel (eds.), Praktiken der (Im-)Mobilisierung. Lager, Sammelunterkünfte und Ankerzentren im Kontext von Asylregimen, Bielefeld: transcript, pp. 183–200.

Adloff, Frank (2021): "Konvivialismus als öffentliche Soziologie.", in: Stefan Selke/Oliver Neun/Robert Jende/Stephan Lessenich/Heinz Bude (eds.), Handbuch Öffentliche Soziologie, Öffentliche Wissenschaft und gesellschaftlicher Wandel, Wiesbaden: Springer, pp. 1–9.

Adloff, Frank/Heins, Volker M. (2015): "Einleitung. Was könnte Konvivialismus sein?", in: Ebd. (eds.), Konvivialismus. Eine Debatte, Bielefeld: transcript, pp. 9–20.

Adloff, Frank/Leggewie, Claus (eds.) (2014): Les convivialistes: Das konvivialistische Manifest. Für eine neue Kunst des Zusammenlebens, Bielefeld: transcript.

Afeworki Abay, Robel/Schmitt, Caroline (2022): "Die Kolonialität der Klimakrise.", in: Tino Pfaff/Barbara Schramkowski/Ronald Lutz (eds.), Klimakrise, sozialökologischer Kollaps und Klimagerechtigkeit: Spannungsfelder für Soziale Arbeit, Weinheim: Beltz Juventa, pp. 206–215.

Afeworki Abay, Robel/Wechuli, Yvonne (2022): "We are here, because you were there: Necropolitics as a Critical Framework for Analysing the Complex Relationship between Colonialism, Forced Migration and Disability.", in: Aida Delic/Ioannis Kourtis/Olga Kytidou/Sabrina Sarkodie-Gyan/Uta Wagner/Janina Zölch (eds.), Globale Zusammenhänge, lokale Deutungen: Kritische Positionierungen zu wissenschaftlichen und medialen Diskursen im Kontext von Flucht und Asyl, Wiesbaden: VS, pp. 25–36.

Anderson, Bridget (2013): Us and them?: The dangerous politics of immigration control. Oxford: Oxford University Press.

Brand, Ulrich/Wissen, Markus (2017): Imperiale Lebensweise. Zur Ausbeutung von Mensch und Natur im globalen Kapitalismus, Munich: Oekom.

Brand, Ulrich/Wissen, Markus (2022): "Imperiale Lebensweise.", in: Daniela Gottschlich/Sarah Hackfort/Tobias Schmitt/Uta von Winterfeld (eds.), Handbuch Politische Ökologie, Bielefeld: transcript, pp. 393–398.

Brizay, Ulrike (2021): "Klimawandel und Migration.", in: Tino Pfaff/Barbara Schramkowski/Ronald Lutz (eds.), Klimakrise, sozialökologischer Kollaps und Klimagerechtigkeit, Weinheim and Basel: Beltz Juventa, pp. 216–228.

Castro Varela, María do Mar (2018): "Das Leiden der Anderen betrachten. Flucht, Solidarität und Postkoloniale Soziale Arbeit", in: Johanna Bröse/Stefan Faas/Barbara Stauber (eds.), Flucht. Herausforderungen für Soziale Arbeit, Wiesbaden: Springer VS, pp. 3–20.

Castro Varela, María do Mar/Mohamed, Sabine (2021): "Intersektionalität und Postkoloniale Soziale Arbeit", in: Astrid Biele Mefebue/Andrea Bührmann/Sabine Grenz (eds.), Handbuch Intersektionalitätsforschung, Wiesbaden: Springer VS, pp. 1–14.

Die konvivialistische Internationale (2020): Das zweite konvivialistische Manifest. Für eine post-neoliberale Welt, Bielefeld: transcript.

Elsen, Susanne (2018): Eco-Social Transformation and Community-Based Economy, London: Routledge.

Felgentreff, Carsten (2015): "Klimaflüchtlinge", in: Sybille Bauriedl (ed.), Wörterbuch Klimadebatte, Bielefeld: transcript, pp. 141–148.

Gutiérrez Rodríguez, Encarnación (2018): "Conceptualizing the coloniality of migration: On European settler colonialism-migration, racism, and migration policies", in: Doris Bachmann-Medick/Jens Kugele (eds.), Migration: Changing Concepts, Critical Approaches, Berlin: de Gruyter, pp. 193–210.

Hickel, Jason (2020): "Quantifying national responsibility for climate breakdown: an equality-based attribution approach for carbon dioxide emissions in excess of the planetary boundary", in: The Lancet Planetary Health 4/9, pp. e399–e404.

Hillmann, Felicitas (2022): Forschungsstand und Forschungsbedarfe zum Zusammenhang von Klimawandel, Migration und Sozialpolitik. Deutsches Institut für Interdisziplinäre Stadtpolitikforschung. https://difis.org/institut/publikationen/publikation/22

Illich, Ivan (1973): Tools for Conviviality, United Kingdom: Marion Boyars Publishers Ltd.

Khoo, Su-ming/Kleibl, Tanja (2020): "Addressing the global emergencies of climate and human rights from below—A view from the pedagogy of development ethics and international social work.", in: Irish Studies in International Affairs 31, pp. 27–42.

Kleibl, Tanja/Lutz, Ronald/Noyoo, Ndangwa (eds.) (2020): The Routledge Handbook of Postcolonial Social Work, London: Routledge.

Lessenich, Stephan (2020): "Doppelmoral hält besser: Die Politik mit der Solidarität in der Externalisierungsgesellschaft.", in: Berliner Journal für Soziologie 30, pp. 113–130.

Liedholz, Yannick (2021a): Soziale Arbeit in Zeiten des Klimawandels: Die Tragödie von Sinzig. https://www.sozial.de/soziale-arbeit-in-zeiten-des-klimawandels-die-tragoedie-von-sinzig.html

Liedholz, Yannick (2021b): Berührungspunkte von Sozialer Arbeit und Klimawandel. Perspektiven und Handlungsspielräume, Opladen, Berlin and Toronto: Barbara Budrich.

Mayblin, Lucy (2017): Asylum after Empire: Colonial Legacies in the Politics of Asylum Seeking, London: Rowman and Littlefield International.

Nixon, Rob (2011): Slow Violence and the Environmentalism of the Poor, London: Harvard University Press.

Or, Yari (2022): "Regenerative Praxis in der Sozialen Arbeit." In: Tino Pfaff/ Barbara Schramkowski/Ronald Lutz (eds.), Klimakrise, sozialökologischer Kollaps und Klimagerechtigkeit, Weinheim and Basel: Beltz Juventa: pp. 248–265.

Peterlini, Hans Karl (2023): "Geteilte Menschheit, geteilte Welt – Grundfragen und Perspektiven für eine friedensorientierte Diversitätspädagogik als Global Citizenship Education." In: Claudia Lohrenscheit/ Andrea Schmelz/Caroline Schmitt/Ute Straub (eds.), Internationale Soziale Arbeit und soziale Bewegungen, Baden-Baden: Nomos (in press).

Schmelz, Andrea (2020): "Klimawandel, globale Migration und ‚Green(ing) Social Work'. Ein ökosozialer und transdisziplinärer Kompass für die internationale Soziale Arbeit.", in: Elke Schwinger (ed.), Das Anthropozän im Diskurs der Fachdisziplinen, Berlin: Metropol Verlag, pp. 39–61.

Spivak, Gayatri C. (2007): "Feminism and human rights", in: Neremeen Shaikh (eds), The present as history: Critical perspectives on global power, New York: Columbia University Press, pp. 172–201.

Statista (2022): Anzahl der Menschen weltweit, die bis zum Jahr 2050 aufgrund des Klimawandels innerhalb ihres Landes/ihrer Region zur Flucht gezwungen werden könnten. https://de.statista.com/statistik/daten/studie/1263402/umfrage/anzahl-moeglicher-klimafluechtlinge-weltweit-bis-2050-nach-region

Weerasinghe, Sanjula (2018): "In harm's way: International protection in the context of nexus dynamics between conflict or violence and disaster or climate change.", in: Legal and Protection Policy Research Series of UNHCR. https://www.unhcr.org/5c1ba88d4.pdf

Wirsching, Sophia (2015): "Klimabedingte Zwangsmigration: Ein Blick aus der Praxis.", in: FluchtforschungsBlog/Forced Migration Studies Blog. https://fluchtforschung.net/blogbeitraege/klimabedingte-zwangsmigration-ein-blick-aus-der-praxis/

World Meteorological Organization (2021): Water-related hazards dominate disasters in the past 50 years. https://public.wmo.int/en/media/press-release/water-related-hazards-dominate-disasters-past-50-years

Climate Crisis, Global Migration, and Disaster Research
Social Work as a Bridging Agent

Malith De Silva, Nishara Fernando, Pia Hollenbach, Marco Krüger, Andrea Schmelz, Caroline Schmitt

The man-made climate crisis has a devastating impact on opportunities and resources of people's wellbeing. Climate induced disasters are major causes of displacement and trigger damages and losses for millions, in particular for poor communities in the Global South. Moreover, a significant, but un-known number of people are forced into displacement as a consequence of slow-onset and cascading disasters (UNDRR/UNU-EHS 2022), caused by climate change such as droughts, cyclones, hurricanes, desertification, rising sea levels and etc. Climate change-induced migration and displacement, environmental degradation and disasters expose communities to high levels of risks (IOM 2020; Schmelz 2019). The International Organization for Migration (IOM) forecasts that by 2050 200 million to 1 billion people will be forced to leave their home due to environmental changes. Moreover, natural and man-made hazards negatively impact over 143 million persons in Africa, Asia and Latin America. According to the Global Report on Internal Displacement (IDMC 2021) climate related disaster events have doubled in the last 20 years due to increase in greenhouse gas emissions. An estimated 7 million people are to be uprooted by disasters (Medina et al. 2022: 75). While there are criticism for the high estimates of impacts of climate change, it is impossible to refute the substantial body of scientific evidence exposing the rapid changes of earths eco and climate systems. People living in the poorest countries are the least responsible for the global warming and environmental crisis, but often suffer the most from lack of coping capacities and a disproportionate disaster exposure (Xu et al. 2020; Markkanen/Anger-Kraavi 2019; Eckstein et al. 2021).

This article has a few key aims: (a) To provide insights into the nexus of climate crisis, climate induced disasters and forced migration, (b) Outlining the role of key stakeholders of climate change adaptation and global governance strategies, (c) Showcasing the role social work can play as a bridging agent between vulnerable people, disaster response and relief services, and the inter/national governance of disasters and relief and rehabilitation efforts, (d) Lastly, the article introduces the international and inter-disciplinary network *Connect4Resilience* formed in 2022 to facilitate, enhance and to call attention to knowledge and practice gaps relevant to climate crises induced social impacts such as forced migration and displacement. The network brings together researchers, practitioners and policy stakeholders to advocate the use of social work to strengthen social science approaches towards climate crisis, inter/national disaster governance and disaster response and relief efforts. The network facilitates co-creation of solution-oriented, transformative and policy relevant knowledge generation. The article concludes with a short outlook.

Climate Crisis, Migration, and Disasters

Global Migration studies reveal that displacement within and across borders in contexts of climate crisis and environmental degradation intersectionally aggravate vulnerabilities of disadvantaged groups, particularly women and children, elderly and people with disabilities (e.g. Balsari et al. 2020; Powers et al. 2018). For instance, disasters increase the risk of all forms of violence—especially gender-based violence, risk of family separation and issues relating to land, housing and property right. Moreover, some vulnerable groups are exposed to multi-dimensional impacts due to forced migration. One such group are children that are forced to migrate. A study by Malith De Silva (2023) reveals that children that were involuntarily relocated experience reduced quality of life due to lack of access to common infrastructure, physical and psychological mistreatment, sexual abuse, social exclusion, reduced access to recreational activities and education. De Silva (2023) further showed that children also suffer due to the challenges and difficulties experienced by parents or guardians such as social exclusion, clashes with host communities and negative impacts on their livelihoods. Furthermore, loss of personal documents undermines overall the access to support services and political rights. Natural and man-made displacement often lead to resettlement or relocation of affected communities. Studies (Fernando 2010; Ruwanpura/ Hollenbach 2013) emphasize that displacement and relocation of individuals exposes them to additional vulnerabilities such as reduced quality of life, disrupting social support networks, increased morbidity, labelling, and social discrimination. Moreover, inter/national displacement and relocation/ resettlement can create a vicious cycle of poverty transferring vulnerabilities and poverty trans-generationally. At the World Climate Conference in November 2022 the Advisory Group on Climate Change and Human Mobility (AGCC) called for immediate action. Both, climate-related sudden- and slow-onset disasters are underpinned by challenges such as unsustainable ecosystems, conflict and war, urbanization, and water shortage. These further increase complex cascading risks. The AGCC describes the current interconnections of climate crisis and global migration as follows (AGCC 2022):

- Climate-induced disasters trigger the flight of millions of people from their homes each year. In 2021, hazardous weather events displaced 22 million individuals. The majority of displaced persons remain in their own country, whereas in other situations displaced leave the country in search of safety.
- Most serious forms of displacement occurs in the Global South, but storms, floods and fires in Australia, Europe and North America also force people in these world regions to flee from their homes. Forced migrants and previously displaced people live under high risks and in extremely vulnerable conditions, suffering mostly from climate emergencies. The same is true for ocean and ocean-dependent communities.

In addition, the 6th Intergovernmental Panel on Climate Change (IPCC 2022) points out that climate change is increasingly responsible for humanitarian crisis in vulnerable contexts. Extreme climate and weather events increase displacement in every part of the world. The IPCC report projects an increase of 200 per cent for human displacement in case of 1.5 °C warming across Africa and a rise of 600 per cent in case of 2.6 °C of warming. These facts and warnings underline the accelerated risks of climate-induced migration and displacement and call for immediate international cooperation with the aim to limit global warming to 1.5 °C related to pre-industrial levels in order to prevent future displacements and risks, involved impacts and socio-economic as well as human costs. IPCC proposes adaptation measures as for example migration, planned relocation and resettlement emphasizing that human-rights based adaptation strategies have to sustainably increase the resilience of individuals and nations, but also reduce vulnerabilities of populations that lack resources to move out of highly risk prone areas. In case displacement cannot be prevented, advanced human-centered and demand-driven planning, technical support and capacity building on various scales need to be offered and promoted within the most affected and risk exposed countries to avoid human, social and economic loss and damage (ibid.).

Global Governance Actors and Strategies

In global governance, climate change adaptation and the mitigation of greenhouse gas emissions are the principal strategies to reduce vulnerabilities regarding climate-related displacement (Mokhnacheva 2022). In the *Sendai Framework of Disaster Risk Reduction* (SFDRR)—the most recent international strategy in that field (UNISDR 2015: 10)—all signing nations recognized that climate-related disasters are a central driver of inter/national displacement. The Sendai Framework (2015–2030) pleads for focused actions within and across sectors at local, national, regional, and global level targeting four priority areas:

(a) understanding disaster risk
(b) disaster risk governance
(c) investing in resilience and
(d) build back better.

With the SFDRR the focus of international governance changed from a narrow perspective of response towards a wider perspective including preventive measures and reduction of existing socio-political and economic vulnerabilities. Therefore, strongly interlinking disaster risk reduction (DRR) with successfully achieving global social and sustainable development as outlined in the Agenda 2030, the Sustainable Development Goals (SDGs) and other relevant international agreements (IOM 2020) highlighting specifically the necessity of needs-driven bottom-up and community-centered approaches. These advancements demonstrate a shift from government to governance and from centralization to decentralization and answer to the increase of "trans-system social ruptures" demanding for more flexibility, adaptiveness and multi-sectoral cooperation (Wachtendorf 2009: 379; IPCC 2012; Pelling 2011). The IOM in particular is engaged in the inclusion of forced migrants in disaster risk management as they often lack access to services, resources and information that affect their lives and security in regular times and in disaster situations. These include for example limited language proficiency, lack of trust in authorities, restriction on mobility, discrimination and racism (Guadagno et al. 2018).

Disasters affect people unequally. Kathleen Tierney (2019) identified racism, gender and class as crucial categories influencing vulnerability. More often than not, these dimensions of vulnerability interact and cause inter-sectional patterns of vulnerabilities (Kuran et al. 2020). The matter is consequently less, *if* a person is vulnerable, but *how* vulnerable a person is. The degree of vulnerability results from the available coping capacity of someone compared to the requirements of a particular situation. In this sense, a person or a group is not per se vulnerable, but might find herself in a vulnerable situation, if the requirements exceed the coping capacities at hand (Gabel 2019). The coping capacities available to communities are not a given, but influenceable. They depend on the recognition of needs and the inclusivity within the society (Krüger 2019). Or in other words: people are not only vulnerable, but are equally made vulnerable in particular situations. This dynamic understanding of vulnerability has become increasingly important in disaster research (Tierney 2019; Wisner et al. 2004). Furthermore, it has found its way into political conceptions of vulnerability. In this sense, the idea of vulnerable situations is presented prominently in the SFDRR and replaced the wording of vulnerable groups that has largely been used in previous international strategies (UNISDR 2015; Krüger/Gabel 2022). This shifting nature of definition is important, since it aids to better understand that it is a political duty to reduce vulnerability by providing the means—financial, political and social—to be able to cope with particular situations and challenges.

Bearing Tierney's dimensions of disaster vulnerability in mind, all forms of involuntary migration and particularly displacement is suited to increase the vulnerability of affected people. People who are forced to move lose their social networks, in many cases—if at all—they have only limited economic capital at their disposal and need to navigate through a relatively new and risk exposed environment. Depending on their legal status, migrants might face restrictions with regard to their access to public services or might hesitate to make use of them (e.g., in the case of undocumented migrants or asylum seekers; see: Tierney 2019: 160–162). Particularly social and economic capital, and also the legal status and cultural capital are crucial factors determining disaster resilience (Aldrich/Meyer 2015; Krüger 2019). Therefore, climate-related disasters not only cause migration, but also affect large parts of the migrant population disproportionally.

The multitude of global governance mechanisms demonstrate the international awareness of the precarious situation of people who are affected by climate-induced displacement and migration. The *Nansen Initiative Agenda for the Protection of Cross-Border Displaced Persons in the Context of Disasters and Climate Change* ("Nansen Protection Agenda") addresses the need for a more coherent approach to the protection of people displaced across borders in the context of disasters and climate change. It was endorsed by 109 countries including the European Union. The successor of the Nansen Initiative is the Platform on Disaster Displacement (disasterdisplacement.org).

Also, the *United Nations Secretary General's High Level Panel on Internal Displacement* was initiated in September 2021. In June 2022, the *United Nations Secretary General's Action Agenda on Internal Displacement* got established. Both agencies address internal displacement proactively in order to strengthen assistance to internally displaced people and to prioritize prevention and durable solutions[1].

Social Work as Bridging Agent

The thesis of this paper is that social work has a central role to play in global governance of disaster management and building resilience. The mandate of social work is the creation of inclusion, social justice and solidarity. All of these factors enhance the resilience of marginalized and deprived people. More than ever, social work is needed as a component of disaster relief.

---

1 https://internaldisplacement-panel.org

Such an approach has been widely discussed internationally, for example in the context of Green Social Work (Dominelli 2012). Lena Dominelli sees an engagement with disasters not as a specific subfield of social work, but as central to it. For this purpose, she developed the *Green Social Work Model* and identified social workers as advocacy workers and awareness builders in the event and beyond the event of disaster. Preventive, eco-social approaches play a central role in her concept (Schmelz 2021). Moreover, another attribute of social work strengthens the proposition to integrate social work in climate change adaptation and disaster management. This attribute is the central role of social work in the case of vulnerable communities. Accordingly, social work considers and treats service users as experts. Therefore, services offered to vulnerable communities are tailor made, community-centered, and bottom-up. Therefore, the resolutions are capable of addressing the specific needs, demands and requirements of vulnerable communities. Therefore, by employing social work as a central player to cope with impacts of climate crisis disaster relief and services aimed at displaced communities can be sensitive to unique characteristics of affected groups. By doing so, social work contributes to the development of community-centric policies and regulations, in other words: social work has an unique ability to bring a bottom up approach to policy formation and implementation in disaster governance and disaster risk reduction.

In German-speaking Europe in particular, this approach has so far been little established (Treptow 2007, 2018; Bähr 2014; Schmitt 2021). In order to further anchor social work as a key player of global disaster relief, we propose an understanding of social work as a *bridging agent* (Hollenbach et al. 2022). Recent disasters highlighted the value of social work as a linking partner and bridging agent working at the frontline of complex social vulnerabilities to decision- and policy-makers of disaster management and governance. Even so, social work practice has proven to be an important and relevant stakeholder, the profession has not yet found its position within the field of disaster management, disaster governance and policy making on global level. Reducing social work to a social-welfare issue for everyday life deprives it from its potential to increase disaster resilience in marginalized societal groups. This is important to mitigate the calamitous consequences of climate-induced hazards. Moreover, it strengthens the resilience of the whole society through improved and better coping and adaptation strategies regarding complex vulnerabilities.

The *Connect4Resilience* Network

In order to bring together social work capacities and to make it visible also towards and in exchange with other disciplines and professions, the „*Connect4Resilience* Network"[2] was founded in 2022 and is financially supported by the Swiss National Science Foundation (SNF). The network was founded by contacting individual members who were already working on the topic of social work as an agent of disaster relief in Switzerland, Germany, Austria, Sri Lanka, Great Britain, Estonia and the US, and expanded internationally including interested colleagues from various disciplines and backgrounds. It understands itself as a network of action-oriented researchers and knowledge brokers continuously aiming for better understanding and building bridges between theory, practice, and policy in the field of social work, disaster research and aid governance. As Margareta Wahlstrom (2017), former Special Representative of the UN Secretary-General for Disaster Risk Reduction (DRR) notes:

> "Social Work and DRR policy share common ground [...]. There is nothing natural about a disaster itself [...] it is the product of risk, which is in turn rooted in a combination of factors, ranging from human behavior and vulnerability, e.g. bad policy decisions and environmental degradation" (ibid.: 334).

Therefore, we do understand research as part of the larger global project achieving the SDG-Agenda 2030 and Sendai Framework of Disaster Risk Reduction. The starting point is to deepen knowledge production and bringing together individuals and institutions of different backgrounds to co-create new knowledge, stronger networks and partnerships supporting the societal and political transformation towards a more disaster resilient, disaster prepared and sustainable society. The overall aim is to connect various stakeholders from research, policy, practice, and society to:

---

2 *Applicants*: Pia Hollenbach & Monika Götzö; *Coordination*: Pia Hollenbach, Monika Götzö & Caroline Schmitt. *Further members*: Dilanthi Amaratunga, Victor Chikadzi, Malith De Silva, Swetha Rao Dhananka, Nishara Fernando, Olivia Frigo-Charles, Melanie Gall, Lauri Goldkind, Anke Kaschlik, Marco Krüger, Noel Muridzo, Kristi Nero, Jana Posmek, Andrea Schmelz, Katharina Wezel.

1. better prepare and plan for future disasters and crises;
2. better integrate and establish knowledge and implementation capacities for resilient and sustainable DRR planning and doing;
3. build capacity and create awareness of the role of social work and social services in disaster contexts;
4. foster societal transformation on various scales to support the achievement of the SDG-Agenda 2030.

Conclusion

The paper provided a comprehensive insight in to the nexus between climate crisis, disasters, and international and internal (forced) migration movements. Social work and disaster management still seem to be separated spheres. However, social work is able to reduce disaster vulnerability by increasing coping capacities at various scales. It is a means to prevent that migrants being treated as passive vulnerable objects, since social work aims at increasing the scope for action. Therefore, it takes the agency of the affected people seriously and therewith contributes to fostering resilience.

To further strengthen and integrate social work approaches in disaster governance and management and to promote an inter-disciplinary and inter-professional exchange, the network *Connect4Resilience* was founded. We neither promote social work as a panacea against vulnerability, nor do we want to see social work structures being made responsible for resilience-building. However, we want to emphasize the potential of social work as a bridging agent and to showcase the importance of adopting and developing the socio-political and financial requirements for social work practice to live up to its potential within disaster governance and management. We would be pleased if colleagues are interested in joining our network and contact one or several of the network members.

References

Advisory Group on Climate Change and Human Mobility (AGCC) (2022): COP 27 Must Act on Human Mobility. https://disasterdisplacement.org/portfolio-item/cop27-must-act-on-human-mobility (30/01/2023).

Aldrich, Daniel P./Meyer, Michelle A. (2015). "Social Capital and Community Resilience", in: American Behavioral Scientist 59/2, pp. 254–269.

Bähr, Christiane (2014): "Katastrophenhilfe – eine Herausforderung für die Soziale Arbeit", in: Christiane Bähr/Hans Günther Homfeldt/Wolfgang Schröer/Cornelia Schweppe (eds.), Weltatlas Soziale Arbeit. Jenseits aller Vermessungen, Weinheim and Basel: Beltz Juventa, pp. 109–123.

Balsari, S./Dresser, C./Leaning, J. (2020): "Climate Change, Migration, and Civil Strife", in: Current Environmental Health Reports 7, pp. 404–414.

De Silva, Malith (2023): Impact of disaster induced displacement and involuntary relocation on children; A case study of Galle, Sri Lanka, University of Colombo (unpublished paper).

Dominelli, Lena (2012): Green Social Work. From Environmental Crisis to Environmental Justice, Cambridge and Malden: Polity Press.

Eckstein, David/Künzel, Vera/Schäfer, Laura (2021): The global climate risk index 2021, Bonn: Germanwatch.

Gabel, Friedrich (2019): "Chancen dynamischer Konzeptionen von Vulnerabilität für den Katastrophenschutz", in: Marco Krüger/Matthias Max (eds.), Resilienz im Katastrophenfall: Konzepte zur Stärkung von Pflege- und Hilfsbedürftigen im Bevölkerungsschutz, Bielefeld: transcript, pp. 77–96.

Guadagno, Lorenzo/Fuhrer, Mechthilde/Twigg, John (eds.) (2018): Migrants in Disaster Risk Reduction. Practices for Inclusion, Geneva: IOM.

Hollenbach, Pia/Goetzoe, Monika/De Silva, Malith (2022): Situating social work within disaster governance. Assessing the agency of social work as a bridging agent and its professionalization in disaster governance. Rio Journal 8.

Hollenbach, Pia/Goetzoe, Monika (2022): Hidden Actors in Covid-19 Emergency Support. In: ALERT Journal 14/2, pp. 17–29.

IOM (2020): IOM and the Sendai Framework: A Global Review of IOM's Contributions to Strengthening Disaster Resilience, Geneva: IOM.

IPCC (2012): Managing the risks of extreme events and disasters to advance climate change adaptation. A Special Report of Working Groups I and II of the Intergovernmental Panel on Climate Change, New York: Cambridge University Press.

IPCC (2022): Climate Change 2022: Impacts, Adaptation and Vulnerability Working Group II Contribution to the Sixth Assessment Report of the Intergovernmental Panel on Climate Change, New York: Cambridge University Press.

Krüger, Marco (2019): "Building Instead of Imposing Resilience: Revisiting the Relationship Between Resilience and the State", in: International Political Sociology 13/1, pp. 53–67.

Krüger, Marco/Gabel, Friedrich (2022): "From Lisbon to Sendai: Responsibilities in International Disaster Management", in: Hannes Hansen-Magnusson/Antje Vetterlein (eds.), The Routledge Handbook on Responsibility in International Relations, Oxon: Routledge, pp. 203–216.

Kuran, Christian H.A. et al. (2020): "Vulnerability and vulnerable groups from an intersectionality perspective", in: International Journal of Disaster Risk Reduction 50, pp. 1–8.

Markkanen, Sanna/Anger-Kraavi, Annela (2019): "Social impacts of climate change mitigation policies and their implications for inequality", in: Climate Policy 19/7, pp. 827–844.

Medina, Catherine K. et al. (2022): Climate Crisis and forced migration. A global social work response for migrants on the move. In: Madhanagopal, Devendraraj/Nikku, Bala R. (eds.), Social work and climate justice: International perspectives, pp. 71–88.

Mokhnacheva, Daria (2022): Baseline Mapping of the Implementation of Commitments related to Addressing Human Mobility Challenges in the Context of Disasters, Climate Change and Environmental Degradation under the Global Compact for Safe, Orderly and Regular Migration (GCM), Geneva: Platform on Disaster Displacement.

Pelling, Mark (2011): "Urban governance and disaster risk reduction in the Caribbean: the experiences of Oxfam GB", in: Environment and Urbanization 23/2, pp. 383–400.

Powers, Meredith C.F. et al. (2018): "Environmental Migration: Social Work at the Nexus of Climate Change and Global Migration", in: Advances in Social Work 18, pp. 1023–1040.

Ruwanpura, Kanchana N./Hollenbach, Pia (2014): "From compassion to the will to improve: Elision of scripts? Philanthropy in post-tsunami Sri Lanka", in: Geoforum 51, pp. 243–251.

Schmelz, Andrea (2019): "Klimawandel, globale Migration, Green(ing) Social Work", in: Elke Schwinger (eds.), Das Anthopozän im interdisziplinären Diskurs, Berlin: Metropol Verlag, pp. 39–61.

Schmelz, Andrea (2021): "Green Social Work für eine post-pandemische Welt: Klimakrise, Covid-19 und das Anthropozän.", in: Ronald Lutz/Jan Steinhaußen/Johannes Kniffki (eds.), Corona, Gesellschaft und Soziale Arbeit. Neue Perspektiven und Pfade, Weinheim and Basel: Beltz Juventa, pp. 220–233.

Schmitt, Caroline (2021): "Soziale Arbeit als Katastrophenhilfe. Perspektiven für eine 'konviviale Weltgemeinschaft'?", in: Ronald Lutz/Jan Steinhaußen/Johannes Kniffki (eds.), Corona, Gesellschaft und Soziale Arbeit. Neue Perspektiven und Pfade, Weinheim and Basel: Beltz Juventa, pp. 234–248.

Tierney, Kathleen (2019): Disasters: A Sociological Approach, Cambridge, Medford: Polity Press.

Treptow, Rainer (2018): "Katastrophenhilfe und humanitäre Hilfe", in: Hans-Uwe Otto/Hans Thiersch/Rainer Treptow/Holger Ziegler (eds.), Handbuch Soziale Arbeit. 6. Ed., München: Ernst Reinhardt, pp. 747–755.

Treptow, Rainer (ed.) (2007): Katastrophenhilfe und Humanitäre Hilfe, München: Ernst Reinhardt.

UNISDR (2015): Sendai Framework for Disaster Risk Reduction 2015–2030. https://www.preventionweb.net/files/43291_sendaiframeworkfordrren.pdf retrieved 09/02/2023.

UNDRR/UNU-EHS (2022): Understanding and managing cascading and systemic risks: lessons from COVID-19, Geneva and Bonn: UNDRR and UNU-EHS.

Wachtendorf, Tricia (2009): "Trans-system social ruptures: exploring issues of vulnerability and resiliency", in: Review of Policy Research 4/26, pp. 379–93.

Wahlstrom, Margareta (2017): "Social work and the Sendai Framework for Disaster Risk Reduction", in: European Journal of Social Work 20/3, pp. 333–336.

Wisner, Ben/Blaikie, Piers/Cannon, Terry/Davis, Ian (2004): At risk: Natural hazards, people's vulnerability and disasters (2. ed.), London u.a.: Routledge.

Xu, Chi/Kohler, Timothy A./Lenton, Timothy M./Svenning, Jens-Christian/ Scheffer, Marten (2020): "Future of the human climate niche", in: Proceedings of the National Academy of Sciences 117/21, pp. 11350–11355.

Migration in a Changing Climate
What Role Can Migrants' Remittances Play in Innovative Financing for the Clean Energy Transition?

Eva Mach, Mariam Traore Chazalnoël, Dina Ionesco

Ever since the Industrial Revolution, energy use and access to energy have shaped the way people move. As hydro and steam power replaced human and animal power, many people migrated from rural areas towards new industrial centers, hereby creating transformative and durable societal changes that still shape our contemporary societies. The nexus between migration and energy is an emerging field of study at research and policy level, but the lack of empirical evidence and academic research on the topic impedes policymakers' ability to develop and implement solutions to observed challenges. In that perspective, this paper seeks to ignite a discussion on a specific dimension of migration—remittances—and the clean energy transition with a special focus on displacement. This article uses the definition of migrants and diaspora as proposed by the International Organization for Migration (IOM) (Sironi et al. 2019: 132–133).[1]

---

1 According to IOM Glossary, migrant is an umbrella term, not defined under international law, reflecting the common lay understanding of a person who moves away from his or her place of usual residence, whether within a country or across an international border, temporarily or permanently, and for a variety of reasons. The term includes a number of well-defined legal categories of people, such as migrant workers; persons whose particular types of movements are legally defined, such as smuggled migrants; as well as those whose status or means of movement are not specifically defined under international law, such as international students. Diaspora are migrants or descendants of migrants whose identity and sense of belonging, either real or symbolic, have been shaped by their migration experience and background. They maintain links with their homelands, and to each other,

Key Migration Trends

An estimated 12 percent of the world's population is either an international or internal migrant. In 2020, this represented around 281 million people living outside of their country of origin (McAuliffe/Triandafyllidou 2021). If current trends continue, the number of international migrants could reach 400 million by 2050 (IOM 2017:2). It is harder to estimate the number of people on the move within their own countries, but a report from 2009 indicated that at the time, at least 740 million people were internal migrants (UNDP 2009: 55). Global trends like increased urbanization and overall population growth are expected to fuel the growth of internal migration in the decades ahead, as close to 70% of the world's population is projected to live in urban areas by 2050 (UNDESA 2019: 1).

If most people move of their own accord, a significant minority is forced into leaving their habitual places of residence. In 2021, forced migration as a result of persecution, armed conflict or generalized violence was at a record high with 89.3 million individuals living in displacement in different contexts. Out of these 89.3 million people, 27.1 million were refugees[2] residing outside of their countries of origin, 4.6 million were seeking asylum, and another 53.2 million were internally displaced people (IDPs)[1] within their own countries (UNCHR 2022). Other estimates confirm that more people are internally displaced worldwide than ever, with estimates of 59.1 million forced to move because of conflict, violence and disasters linked to natural hazards (IDMC 2022: 12)[3].

---

based on a shared sense of history, identity, or mutual experiences in the destination country. Sironi, Alice/Bauloz, Céline/Emmanuel, Milen (eds.) (2019) : "Glossary on Migration." In International Migration Law, No. 34, pp 132–133. https://publications.iom.int/system/files/pdf/iml_34_glossary.pdf

2   A refugee is a person who, "owing to a well-founded fear of persecution for reasons of race, religion, nationality, membership of a particular social group or political opinions, is outside the country of his nationality and is unable or, owing to such fear, is unwilling to avail himself of the protection of that country. (Art. 1(A)(2), Convention relating to the Status of Refugees, Art. 1A (2), 1951 as modified by the 1967 Protocol).

3   The internationally recognized Guiding Principles on Internal Displacement define IDPs as: persons or groups of persons who have been forced or obliged to fee or to leave their homes or places of habitual residence, in particular as a result of or in order to avoid the effects of armed conflict, situations of generalized violence, violations of human rights or natural

Displacement linked to disasters has become increasingly visible, with examples such as floods and droughts, displacing nearly 1.4 million people in Afghanistan since 2018 (IDMC 2022: 12). While conflicts and violence have led to the internal displacement of 7.6 million people per year on average between 2008 and 2017, disasters have been displacing three times more people, with an average of 24.6 million people per year (IDMC 2019: 6). This trend is likely to continue as the effects of climate change are predicted to intensify and increase the frequency of both extreme weather and climate events. Furthermore, it is likely that significant numbers of people are also on the move across international borders due to disasters and climate impacts, but consolidated estimates on these kinds of movements are not available. Finally, more subtle environmental disruptions linked to slow-onset climatic change also impact both internal and international migration (Traore Chazalnoël/ Randall 2021: 5–7). As economic means of livelihoods are negatively affected by slow onset change, for instance the degradation of land used for pastures and agriculture or ocean acidification in areas where fishing represents a primary source of income, the number of people on the move in the coming decades might increase further.

In addition to conflicts and disasters, millions of people are also displaced due to infrastructural projects often linked to energy provision. Even if exact estimates are not available, some incidents outline however the scope of the issue. For example, in 2017, the Internal Displacement Monitoring Center estimated that 80 million people had been displaced by dam construction only (IDMC 2017: 2).

The mining industry is another example of a double edge sword when it comes to migration and the energy transition. As the world struggles to replace fossil fuel sources with renewables, current debates highlight the "dual role of the mining industry as both a negative impactor and a supplier of energy transition metals (ETMs) that are crucial for climate change mitigation" (Svobodova et al. 2020: 4). According to a World Bank study, over a 1000% rise in minerals supply is needed for energy storage technologies under a 2 degrees climate scenario (World Bank 2017: 35). These minerals include aluminum, cobalt, iron, lead, lithium, manganese, and nickel—and the impacts of their extraction on migration are complex.

---

or human-made disasters, and who have not crossed an internationally recognized State border (United Nations, 1998 (E/CN.4/1998/53/Add.2).

Migration in the mining sector includes a wide variety of mobility patterns, however the linkages to the clean energy transitions have not yet been fully explored. An ILO report on the topic noted that the number of migrants moving to work in mines is uncertain, especially as "the mining industry is a sector in which direct employment multiplies indirectly the number of jobs created and these are at times and, in certain circumstances, likely to be filled by migrants from neighboring countries" (Coderre-Proulx/Campbel/ Mandé 2016: ix).

On the one hand, increased mining activities can provide a push factor for people to move as they search for livelihood opportunities working in mines or around its support infrastructures. For example, international migrants work in nickel mines such Chinese migrant workers in the Ramu Nickel mine in Papua New Guinea or Filipino migrant workers in the Koniambo mine in New Caledonia (Coderre-Proulx/Campbel/Mandé 2016: 47–55).

On the other hand, it is widely acknowledged that mine development-related displacement, relocation, and resettlement pose significant social risk (Owen/Kemp 2015: 486), as outlined in debates on environmental justice (Temper/del Bene/Martinez-Alier 2015: 272). However, displacement and resettlement as part of the unintended consequences of the clean energy transition have not been sufficiently studied and integrated into policy making. Evaluating the migration costs versus the benefits in terms of raw materials needed for the clean energy is potentially a loaded public policy issue with no easy answers. While some resettled communities report positive relocation experiences, many communities suffer through coercive measures and are forced to move due to mining (Rüttinger et al. 2020: 20). Mining also impacts the availability and accessibility of natural resources in the area of operations which can in return impact people's decision to migrate as their livelihoods and vital space shrink. In any case, these examples demonstrate the clear link between mining and migration as an important area to consider in the clean energy transition and climate justice debates.

Migration is a dynamic phenomenon that defies at times classification. Traditionally, migration literature distinguished between forced and voluntary forms of migration. Yet, for example in migration linked to slow onset climate impacts, it is becoming harder to determine how voluntary migration is, as people usually move out of degraded areas in anticipation of or to adapt to worsening conditions. On the ground, migration realities are nuanced, and multiple realities coexist in the same space. The concept of mixed migration refers to migration flows where both voluntary and forced migrants travel on the same routes and means of transportation (Sironi et al. 2019: 141). This concept also acknowledges that people usually move due to a combination of factors: economic, political, social and environmental (Sironi et al. 2019: 142). For example, in the case of the Lake Chad Basin, political drivers, such as protracted conflict, combined with environmental factors, such as drought, come together to drive people to migrate.

Millions of people are already migrating, many in search of or due to basic services, like energy needs. Millions more people are expected to be on the move in the coming decades, especially due to climate change impacts (Viviane et al. 2021: xv). These people, like any others, have energy needs that needs to be met to ensure their wellbeing, safety, human rights and access to economic development.

Why Is Migration Important When Discussing the Clean Energy Transition?

The link between migration and energy is complex, partly due to the fluid nature of migration flows as described above. However, both migration and energy policymakers agree on the need to examine these linkages and propose a wide range of integrated policy and operational solutions that respond to a large spectrum of observed challenges, including the following:

1. Access to and availability of energy sources can drive fully or in part people's decision to migrate. For instance, a case study in Nepal suggests that access to affordable, reliable, and clean energy services can alleviate poverty and accelerate development in rural areas, which in turn can lower the rate of out-migration from rural areas (Zahnd 2013).
2. Climate change mitigation policies can displace people from their homes and land, for example through the development of large-scale renewable energy solutions and mining activities that are needed to make clean energy technologies. The exact magnitude of such development-induced displacement is currently unknown, but it is estimated that millions of people per year are forced to migrate due to infrastructure constructions and mining.

3. At the same time, the development of large-scale renewable energy solutions can improve livelihoods and standards of living conditions, and therefore reduce forced migration as people are better able to live fulfilling lives in their areas of origin. Some empirical studies outline that development and poverty reduction impact migration patterns through access to energy. For instance, the Government of Brazil evaluated the impact of electrification in rural settings and found that rural out-migration was reversed after access to modern energy services was improved, with 5% of migrants returning to their communities of origin. It also found that 1.7% of the households who intended to migrate decided to stay following the provision of energy services (Government of Brazil 2013).

4. People in transit towards their final destinations also have specific energy needs. For instance, in migrant transit centers, reliable access to energy is needed to ensure that people can cook and have access to water supplies or communicate with their families and communities.

5. Energy access for displaced populations is essential at different levels: to ensure basic survival (cooking, heating, cooling, etc.), lessen protection issues and safeguard human dignity (access to adequate WASH facilities, improved safety in camps through lighting), and promote long-term development that will benefit both mobile and host populations.

6. Large-scale movements of people can put pressure on access to and availability of energy sources. Competition to access energy resources might create tensions and social unrest in the community. In situations where large numbers of displaced are housed in camps settings, governments and humanitarian agencies might struggle to ensure that energy needs are met due to lack of infrastructure and funding. In situations where people migrate or are displaced into communities, their presence can put pressure on existing energy infrastructure and increase the cost of services. For instance, the large numbers of Syrian refugees in the Hashemite Kingdom of Jordan increased the overall energy needs in the country. As a result, the Jordanian Government pioneered the Jordan Response Platform for the Syria Crisis (JRPSC), a model bringing together the existing refugee response and national development planning under one national planning and coordination framework. Access to energy is one of the sectoral priorities under the JRPs, with a clear articulation of need and budgetary estimations to address this issue. The JRPSC illustrates

how humanitarian response can be better aligned with development objectives to ensure that the energy needs of displaced people and host communities are comprehensively accounted for (Huber/Mach 2019).

7. Even when energy is available and accessible, energy sources available to migrants might not be clean and can create further environmental damage, for instance, deforestation. This is most evident in the case of firewood fuel collection in Sub-Saharan African countries where refugee populations do not have access to or cannot afford alternative fuel supplies (Cross et al. 2019: 22–24).

One of the key public policy issues is therefore how to ensure that mobile populations have access to clean energy, at all stages of their migration journeys (before departure, while on the move and once they arrive at destination). This enormous endeavor can only be achieved by large scale investments in climate mitigation measures, strong partnerships with private energy specialists and the systematic consideration of migration dimensions in energy and development policy.

However, government-led efforts can be complemented by those of migrants themselves. For millions, migration is a positive experience that allow people to improve their standards of living, access to education and general wellbeing. Migrants' communities established abroad have a long tradition of providing financial and technological support to their communities and families who remained in their places of origin. Diasporas and migrants abroad have long been recognized as agents of development, but their role in climate action and renewabl²e energy access remain underexplored.

Remittances—A Potential Source for Blended Finance

One of the key benefits of migration, remittances represent a vital support for millions of people worldwide. In 2020, worldwide remittance flows to low- and middle-income countries amounted to 540 billion dollars (World Bank 2022a), compared to the total global official development assistance (ODA) at 162.17 billion dollars (OECD 2021). As such, migrant contributions in the form of remittances were more than three times more than ODA from official donor countries. Remittance flows are likely to be much higher when informal channels are included beyond the officially recorded data.

At the household level, they complement income needed to meet immediate needs such as getting and sustaining access to basic services, including food, shelter, water and sanitation, education, and health care. All these services necessitate reliable and sustainable access to energy to function properly. Remittances can also help cope with decreasing income levels in times of crisis, which is becoming increasingly relevant in the light of more severe and more frequent weather-related disasters linked to climate change and a post-COVID 19 world threatened by recurring pandemics.

The United Nations (UN) estimates that around three quarters of remittances are used to cover essential things and services (UNDESA Undated). The rest—representing over 100 billion dollars every year globally—can be either saved or invested in longer-term development, such as assets that increase standards of living or activities that generate income. Once basic needs are met, remittances can be leveraged for community projects aimed to increase quality of life and sustain livelihoods, for example through establishing and increasing access to water, sanitation and hygiene or energy services (UNDESA Undated).

Excluding China, remittance flows have been the largest source of external finance for low- and middle-income countries since 2015, including in countries where the largest numbers of internally displacement persons (IDPs) and refugees live (World Bank 2022b: 9). For instance, the African continent accounts for more than a third of the world's displaced people (NRC 2022) and many countries receive billions of dollars yearly in remittances. Remittance inflows to Sub-Saharan Africa increased to 49 billion dollars in 2021, with Nigeria, the largest remittance recipient country in the region, receiving 19.2 billion dollars in remittances in 2021 while the Democratic Republic of Congo received 1.3 billion. In 2020, remittances as a share of gross domestic product (GDP) were the highest in Somalia and South Sudan. Another example, Ukraine before the 2022 war received 15 billion dollars in remittances, or 9.9% of its GDP (World Bank 2022a).

This has potentially tremendous implications for energy policy makers. Since finance is key to sustainable development, climate action and the energy transition, more thinking should be done on how migration and remittances can support the energy transition in low- and middle-income countries and contribute to transforming the lives of communities in countries of origin that are affected by large-scale displacement.

The transformative power of regulated remittance investments in clean energy was recognized in the early 2000s (IADB 2009). The RemitEnergy project for example was launched to help channel remittances from the US-based Haitian diaspora to finance renewable energy projects in Haiti (RemitEnergy 2021). This business model was piloted in 2012 in Haiti and proved that remittances can be a viable means to finance and/or co-finance clean energy projects. Since 2009, the RemitEnergy model has also been implemented in Bolivia with migrant workers living in Spain financing solar water boilers for their communities of origin (RemitEnergy 2021).

However, while studies on the impact of remittances on economic growth are widely available, evidence focusing on the linkages between remittances and energy are scarce (Akçay/Demirtaş 2015). One of the available empirical studies was conducted in Bangladesh, one of the largest refugee hosting countries, by Das et al. (2021). This study found that increased remittance inflows to Bangladesh generated additional demand for modern renewable technology such as solar home systems, and therefore contributed to national energy transition efforts.

Existing examples suggest that remittances can help increase access to energy services and support the clean energy transition in countries of origin, including in countries that experience large-scale displacement and populations' movements. However, more research and evidence are needed to bring this nexus to the attention of policy makers, increase confidence in the validity of this model and encourage the development of programs and policies that help increase the use of remittances to support clean energy access.

Diaspora Bonds—Financing Investment at the National Level

One of the specific policy measures that can be developed to leverage remittances for energy access and the energy transition is the development of diaspora bonds. The Migration Policy Institute defines diaspora bonds as a "government debt security with investors drawn from the country's nationals living abroad, their descendants, or those with another connection to the nation" (Migration Policy Institute 2021). Diaspora bonds are issued by a government with the primary purpose to diversify their investment base and attract alternative financing from their diaspora, often borrowing at below-market rates and during crisis (Idem).

Through diaspora bonds, migrants living abroad invest in national-level projects in a formal and regulated way, unlike remittances that are sent informally to households. According to a World Bank study, diaspora bonds have been successfully used by Israel and India to channel diaspora investments into government-led initiatives. The state of Israel has engaged its diaspora since 1951 to raise 32.4 billion dollars, while India issued diaspora bonds on three occasions to raise 11.3 billion dollars by the early 2000s (Ketkar/Ratha 2007: 2). The same study also examined the situation of several other countries that are potential candidates for issuing diaspora bonds, including those experiencing large-scale displacement and/or low energy access rates, such as Bangladesh, Haiti, Afghanistan, Somalia, Democratic Republic of Congo and Mozambique (Ketkar/Ratha Undated: 3). The potential of such bonds to fund infrastructure projects for the energy transition is clear, but under specific conditions, including additional credit enhancements and investor protection.

Indeed, existing case studies outline some of the risks associated with diaspora bonds for energy infrastructure. On the African continent, Ethiopia pioneered the issuance of diaspora bonds as early as 2008. The money raised through bond issuance was intended to finance a hydroelectric power project of the Ethiopia Electric Power. Another attempt in 2011 focused on increasing energy security through financing the construction of a dam on the Blue Nile. Both initiatives failed to deliver the expected results due to the diaspora's concerns about the high probability of default and the environmental risks related to the power and dam projects. Even if these bonds attracted relatively few investors due to perceived high risks, it is noteworthy that the first attempt to leverage diaspora bonds as a source of finance in Sub-Saharan Africa focused on increasing access to energy. This policy choice highlights how critical energy access is to national development and the need to turn to innovative financing sources to ensure that national energy needs are met.

Other initiatives from the continent have successfully raised finance for infrastructure projects, including for power generation. Kenya issued its first diaspora bond in 2009, raising 164 million euros for transport, energy, and water projects. In 2017 Nigeria, with one of the largest African diaspora populations in the world, launched its diaspora bonds to leverage diaspora finance and raised nearly 300 million dollars to finance the country's budget deficit linked to capital-intensive investment projects (Brookings 2022).

Another policy issue of interest is linked to non-financial remittances and how some migrants' specific expertise and knowledge on energy could complement financial remittances. However, remittances should complement national policy efforts to provide energy access and support the transition towards sustainable energy but not replace these efforts, at the risk of placing a disproportionate burden on individual migrants and diaspora communities. Given the weight of remittances and the perceived wealth of diaspora communities, mobilizing diaspora investments can potentially play a key role in leveraging further investment or co-financing projects in the countries of origin. Such blended finance would merit further research and economic modelling especially for those countries that struggle with underdevelopment, low access to energy rates, high dependency on fossil fuels and the burden of displacement. In that respect, intergovernmental policy discussions are key to increase awareness of this potential and encourage the development of more analysis and evidence to support policy making.

Remittances in Global Policy Discussions

The potential of remittances is acknowledged in many multilateral policy discussions dedicated to migration and conducted among United Nations Member States. Through international policy instruments, such as the 2015 Sustainable Development Goals and the Global Compact for Safe, Orderly and Regular Migration (GCM), the international community recognized the positive role of remittances in socio-economic development and its potential in reducing inequalities within and among countries (Sustainable Development Goal 10).

The necessity to increase the efficiency of remittances and leverage them for sustainable development was reflected in SDG 10.c. target, which focuses on reducing the cost of sending money back home: "By 2030, reduce to less than 3 per cent the transaction costs of migrant remittances and eliminate remittance corridors with costs higher than 5 per cent". At the 2022 High-Level Political Forum on Sustainable Development, Member States recommitted to supporting the implementation of SDG 10.c. and leveraging remittances for sustainable development (United Nations Economic and Social Council 2022: 25).

In 2018, the first global migration policy instrument negotiated among UN Member States reiterated the commitment expressed in SDG 10.c., with Objective 20 of the Global Compact for Migration to *"Promote faster, safer and cheaper transfer of remittances and foster financial inclusion of migrants"*. The GCM looks at the issue of remittances mostly from a financial perspective, and outlines policy actions states can take to optimize financial flows and reduce transaction costs (Basaran/Piper 2018). From an energy perspective, action point 'g' (*Develop programmes and instruments to promote investments from remittance senders in local development and entrepreneurship in countries of origin, such as through matching grant mechanisms, municipal bonds and partnerships with hometown associations, in order to enhance the transformative potential of remittances beyond the individual households of migrant workers at skills levels*) provides an entry point to promote the role of remittances for energy infrastructure development as it considers remittances as a blended finance tool for local development.

In 2022, the first International Migration Review Forum served as the primary intergovernmental global platform to discuss and share progress on the implementation of all aspects of the GCM four years after its adoption. The Progress Declaration resulting from the International Migration Review Forum recognized the crucial role remittances played during the global COVID-19 pandemic, and many countries "eased regulations [...], facilitated greater digitalization, offered incentives and abolished or waived transaction fees" (United Nations 2022). Looking ahead, states committed to redouble efforts to reduce the average transaction cost of remittances to less than 3 percent by 2030, including through the widespread use of digital solutions.

Migration considerations are increasingly discussed in climate policy, notably the annual climate negotiations conducted among United Nations Member States. While the 2015 Paris Agreement does not specifically refer to remittances, broader climate change discussions conducted under the UN climate action agenda and follow-up mechanisms consider the role of remittances, for example, in relation to financing Loss and Damage (Handmer/Nalau 2017: 2). 'Green remittances' have also been explored in Ghana and Burkina Faso as complementary sources of financing for adaptation and mitigation (Ferro 2021, Musah-Surugu et al. 2017). Remittances are important enough to be mentioned in the Nationally Determined Contributions (NDCs), the primary policy instruments translating the global commitment of the Paris Agreement into national level action. Remittance flows have been mentioned in NDCs as 'shrinking' financial resources due to the impact of the COVID-19 pandemic and global recession in the NDC of Somalia (The Federal Republic of Somalia 2021: 1), Ethiopia (Federal Democratic Republic of Ethiopia 2021: 3) and Jordan (Ministry of Environment of the Hashemite Kingdom of Jordan 2021: 6). The NDC of Tajikistan referred to remittances as an enabling tool for poverty eradication and sustainable development (Republic of Tajikistan 2021: 18).

The Glasgow Climate Pact negotiated at the 26th Conference of the Parties in 2021 acknowledged and recalled the commitment of Parties to consider their respective obligations on migrants and consider them when taking climate action (UNFCCC 2022: 2–3). It also called upon Parties "to continue to explore innovative approaches and instruments for mobilizing finance" (UNFCCC 2022: 11). While remittances were not explicitly mentioned, the examples mentioned above demonstrate that they could contribute to innovative financing.

The Addis Ababa Action Agenda of the Third International Conference on Financing for Development dedicated paragraph 40 to remittances, acknowledging the vital role of remittances to "meet part of needs of recipient households" and the need to "ensure that adequate and affordable financial services" to optimize such money transfers and reduce "average transaction cost of migrants". While remittances are not directly mentioned in the context of the energy transition and for displacement settings, the Action Agenda refers to promoting "both public and private investment in energy infrastructure and clean energy technologies" (United Nations 2015: 19).

The role of remittances has also been highlighted in thematic and regional policy discussions. For example, the Small Island Developing States (SIDS) Accelerated Modalities of Action (Samoa Pathway), an international policy instrument focused on sustainable development in SIDS, outlined remittances and "their importance for the economic growth of small island developing States" (United Nations 2014: 10). SIDS are among the most climate vulnerable countries in the world and already experiencing irreversible environmental changes linked to climate change, such as sea-level rise and unpredictable weather patterns, threatening the lives and livelihoods of communities in the Pacific, Caribbean, and Indian Ocean islands. They are also highly reliant on imported fossil fuels, which was also recognized as "major source of economic vulnerability" by the Samoa Pathway (United Nations 2014: 26). Migration, both in economic and forced forms, is already a reality for many of the SIDS. In this complex context, remittances could provide the necessary co-investment needed in climate-resilient infrastructure and locally produced energy. It would also allow to shift away from imported, costly fuel sources, which have been a factor hindering the "growth prospects of the small island developing States" (Idem).

The importance of remittances is acknowledged across major global and regional policy discussions. In turn, these discussions can promote better understanding of the issue and enhance the willingness of states to develop provisions at the national level to lower the cost of remittances and propose specific schemes, such as diaspora bonds, to leverage the use of remittances for national and local development, including energy access and energy provision. However, discussions on the specific link between remittances and clean energy transition are not yet widespread, and there is little emphasis on examining and analyzing lessons learned from existing initiatives in countries that face large-scale displacement. Yet, increased consideration of migration issues in policy areas not traditionally concerned with the topic—notably climate change mitigation and adaptation -, offers the opportunity to enhance awareness of the remittance-energy nexus and analyze the opportunities but also associated risks in forced migration contexts.

Looking Ahead: Starting Small and Privileging Action at the Community Level

Analyzing the development benefits of migration, including of remittances and knowledge transfer, represents a new frontier for research and policy development in the energy transition context. Across the globe, powerful examples demonstrate how remittances can help finance renewable energy technologies and the development of sustainable energy markets in countries of origin of migrants. The very existence of such initiatives and the lessons learnt from their implementation should encourage policymakers to look at how structured, national-level programs, such as diaspora bonds, can help co-finance the energy transition.

Remittances will most likely continue to be used to meet immediate basic needs of recipients, including in terms of access to energy. But the portion of remittances not used to meet immediate needs have a real potential to positively impact local communities, especially in underdeveloped and underfunded displacement settings. While remittances cannot replace climate finance, they can help support climate action if appropriate incentives are provided to channel remittances towards adaptation and mitigation and risks for investors are mitigated (Berdandi/Pauw 2016). Migrants sending remittances back home might have more emotional, financial, and social incentives to invest in energy projects that directly impact their households and communities at the local level. While there is certainly room for ambitious national level schemes to leverage remittances, policymakers might want to increase pilot projects at the community level that directly and immediately benefit households who receive remittances. In that context, leveraging remittances as a blended finance mechanism complemented by public or private sector investment could help quickly set up much needed clean energy projects at the community level, that would in turn improve the daily lives but also the future prospects of households and local communities.

References

Berdandi, Barbara/Pauw, Peter (2016): Remittances for Adaptation: An Alternative Source of International Climate Finance?, Migration, Risk Management and Climate Change: Evidence and Policy Responses, Global Migration issues, Berlin: Springer. https://www.idos-research.de/en/others-publications/article/remittances-for-adaptation-an-alternative-source-of-international-climate-finance/

Coderre-Proulx, Mylène/Campbel, Bonnie/Mandé, Issiaka (2016): International Migrant Workers in the Mining Sector, Geneva: International Labour Organization, pp. 47–55. https://www.ilo.org/wcmsp5/groups/public/---ed_protect/---protrav/---migrant/documents/publication/wcms_538488.pdf

Cross, Jamie et al (2019): Energy and Displacement in Eight Objects: Insights from Sub-Saharan Africa. Moving Energy Initiative pp. 22–24. https://www.chathamhouse.org/2019/11/energy-and-displacement-eight-objects/4-firewood

Das, Anupam/McFarlane, Adian/Carels, Luc (2021): "Empirical exploration of remittances and renewable energy consumption in Bangladesh", in: Asia-Pacific Journal of Regional Science 5, p. 65–89. https://doi.org/10.1007/s41685-020-00180-6

"Diaspora bonds: An innovative source of financing?", 15 December 2022. https://www.brookings.edu/blog/africa-in-focus/2022/05/27/diaspora-bonds-an-innovative-source-of-financing/

Federal Democratic Republic of Ethiopia (2021): Updated Nationally Determined Contribution. https://unfccc.int/sites/default/files/NDC/2022-06/Ethiopia%27s%20updated%20NDC%20JULY%202021%20Submission_.pdf

Ferro, Anna (2021): Making room for green remittances. The role of the diaspora engagement in fighting climate change effects in the origin country: the case study of the community from Burkina Faso in Italy. https://www.cespi.it/sites/default/files/documenti/final_edited_executive_summary_eng_green_remittances_a_ferro.pdf

Figures at a Glance (n.d) United Nations High Commissioner for Refugees (UNHCR). https://www.unhcr.org/figures-at-a-glance.html

"GCM Commentary: Objective 20: Promote faster, safer and cheaper transfer of remittances and foster financial inclusion of migrants", 4 October 2018. https://rli.blogs.sas.ac.uk/2018/10/04/gcm-commentary-objective-20/

Government of Brazil, Ministério de Minas e Energia (2013): '10 years, 15 million beneficiaries: Quantitative household evaluation of satisfaction and impact evaluation of the Light for All program's main results', MME, Brasilia. http://www.mme.gov.br/documents/10584/3042878/Pesquisa+2013/c14eec59-80b6-4276-802f56736b3e03df;jsessionid=6C-7C37690FDF34D0B537CA9EE0DE52ED.srv155

Handmer/John, Nalau/Johanna (2017): Financing Loss and Damage: what is used versus what might happen. A comment for: "Loss & Damage, UNFCCC". https://cop23.unfccc.int/sites/default/files/resource/Financing%20Loss%20and%20Damage_Handmer%26Nalau.pdf

Huber, Suzanna/Mach, Eva (2019). "Policies for increased sustainable energy access in displacement settings", in: Nat Energy 4, 1000–1002. https://doi.org/10.1038/s41560-019-0520-1

Inter-American Development Bank (2009): Financing Sustainable Energy through Remittance Flows in Haiti and the Dominican Republic. https://publications.iadb.org/en/publication/financing-sustainable-energy-through-remittance-flows-haiti-and-dominican-republic

Internal Displacement Monitoring Centre (2019): Disaster Displacement, A global review, 2008–2018, Geneva: IDMC. https://www.internal-displacement.org/publications/disaster-displacement-a-global-review

Internal Displacement Monitoring Centre (2022): GRID [Global Report on Internal Displacement] 2022, Geneva: IDMC, p. 12. https://www.internal-displacement.org/sites/default/files/publications/documents/IDMC_GRID_2022_LR.pdf

Internal Displacement Monitoring Centre (2017): Dam Displacement, Geneva: IDMC, p. 2. https://www.internal-displacement.org/sites/default/files/publications/documents/20170411-idmc-intro-dam-case-study.pdf

Ketkar, Suhas/Ratha, Dilip (2007): Development Finance Via Diaspora Bonds Track Record and Potential. World Bank Policy Research Working Paper No. 4311, p. 2. https://ssrn.com/abstract=1006322

Ketkar, Suhas/Ratha, Dilip (n.d.): Diaspora Bonds for Education, p. 3. https://web.worldbank.org/archive/website01363/WEB/IMAGES/DIASPORA.PDF

Mach, Eva (2019): "The Migration-Energy Nexus in International Policy", in: Grafham, Owen (ed.), Energy Access and Forced Migration, London: Routledge. https://doi.org/10.4324/9781351006941-4

McAuliffe, Marie/Ruhs, Martin (2017): World Migration Report 2018, Geneva: International Organization for Migration, p. 2 http://publications.iom.int/system/files/pdf/wmr_2018_en.pdf

McAuliffe, Marie/Triandafyllidou, Anna (2021): World Migration Report 2022, Geneva: International Organization for Migration. https://world-migrationreport.iom.int/wmr-2022-interactive/

Migration Policy Institute (2021): Can Diaspora Bonds Supercharge Development Investment?, p. 1. https://www.migrationpolicy.org/article/diaspora-bonds-supercharge-development-investment

Ministry of Environment of the Hashemite Kingdom of Jordan (2021): Updated Submission of Jordan's Nationally Determined Contribution, p. 6. https://unfccc.int/sites/default/files/NDC/2022-06/UPDATED%20SUBMISSION%20OF%20JORDANS.pdf

Musah-Surugu, Issah Justice/Ahenkan, Albert/Bawole, Justice Nyigmah/Darkwah, Samuel Antwi (2017): "Migrants' remittances: A complementary source of financing adaptation to climate change at the local level in Ghana", in: International Journal of Climate Change Strategies and Management. https://doi.org/10.1108/IJCCSM-03-2017-0054

Organisation for Economic Co-operation and Development (2021): The global picture of official development assistance (ODA). https://public.tableau.com/views/AidAtAGlance/DACmembers

Owen, John R./Kemp, Deanna (2015): "Mining-induced displacement and re-settlement: a critical appraisal", in: Journal of Cleaner Production, 87, pp. 478–488. p. 486. https://doi.org/10.1016/j.jclepro.2014.09.087

"RemitEnergy: Powering Communities through Remittances", 17 May 2021. https://energy-base.org/news/remitenergy-powering-communities-through-remittances/

"RemitEnergy: Enabling Bolivian Emigrants to Direct Remittances towards Sustainable Energy". https://energy-base.org/projects/remitting-solar-water-heaters-in-bolivia

"Remittances matter: 8 facts you don't know about the money migrants send back home", 17 June 2019. https://www.un.org/development/desa/en/news/population/remittances-matter.html.

"Remittances and the SDGs". https://www.un.org/en/observances/remit-tances-day/SDGs

Republic of Tajikistan (2021): The Updated NDC of the Republic of Tajikistan, p. 18. https://unfccc.int/sites/default/files/NDC/2022-06/NDC_TAJIKISTAN _ENG.pdf

Rüttinger, Lukas et al. (2020): KlimRess—Impacts of climate change on mining, related environmental risks and raw material supply. Case study on PGMs and nickel mining in South Africa, Dessau-Roßlau: Umweltbundesamt, p. 20. https://www.umweltbundesamt.de/sites/default/files/medien/479/publikationen/texte_106-2020_klimress_case_study_south_africa.pdf

Sironi, Alice/Bauloz, Céline/Emmanuel, Milen (eds.) (2019): "Glossary on Migration.", in: International Migration Law, No. 34, pp. 132–133, 141–142. https://publications.iom.int/system/files/pdf/iml_34_glossary.pdf

Svobodova, Kamila et al. (2020): "Complexities and contradictions in the global energy transition: a re-evaluation of country-level factors and dependencies", in: Appl. Energy 265, 114778, p. 4. https://www.nature.com/articles/s41467-020-18661-9

Temper, Leah/del Bene, Daniela/Martinez-Alier, Joan (2015): "Mapping the frontiers and front lines of global environmental justice.", in: Journal of Political Ecology, 22, p. 272. https://doi.org/10.2458/v22i1.21108

The Federal Republic of Somalia (2021): Updated Nationally Determined Contribution, p. 1. https://unfccc.int/sites/default/files/NDC/2022-06/ Final%20Updated%20NDC%20for%20Somalia%202021.pdf

"The world beyond Ukraine—An overview of the world's displacement crises in 2021", 16 June 2022. https://www.nrc.no/the-world-beyond-ukraine

Traore Chazalnoël, Mariam/Randall, Alex (2021): "Migration and the slow-onset impacts of climate change: Taking stock and taking action.", in: McAuliffe, Marie/Triandafyllidou, Anna (eds.), World Migration Report 2022, Geneva: International Organization for Migration (IOM), pp. 5–7. https://publications.iom.int/books/world-migration-report-2022-chapter-9

United Nations (2014): SIDS Accelerated Modalities of Action (SAMOA) Pathway, pp. 10 and 26. https://documents-dds-ny.un.org/doc/UNDOC/GEN/ N14/628/45/PDF/N1462845.pdf?OpenElement

United Nations (2015): Addis Ababa Action Agenda of the Third International Conference on Financing for Development (Addis Ababa Action Agenda) pp. 19. https://www.un.org/esa/ffd/wp-content/uploads/2015/08/AAAA_ Outcome.pdf

United Nations (2022): Progress Declaration of the International Migration Review Forum, p. 8. https://migrationnetwork.un.org/system/files/ docs/A%20AC.293%202022%20L.1%20English.pdf

United Nations Economic and Social Council (2022): Ministerial declaration of the high-level segment of the 2022 session of the Economic and Social Council and the 2022 high-level political forum on sustainable development, convened under the auspices of the Council, on the theme "Building back better from the coronavirus disease (COVID-19) while advancing the full implementation of the 2030 Agenda for Sustainable Development". p. 25. https://digitallibrary.un.org/record/3986168?ln=en

United Nations Framework Convention on Climate Change (2022): Report of the Conference of the Parties serving as the meeting of the Parties to the Paris Agreement on its third session, held in Glasgow from 31 October to 13 November 2021, pp. 2, 3, 11. https://unfccc.int/sites/default/files/resource/cma2021_10_add1_adv.pdf

United Nations, Department of Economic and Social Affairs, Population Division (2017): International Migration Report 2017: Highlights (ST/ ESA/SER.A/404), New York: United Nations, p. 1. http://www.un.org/en/

development/desa/population/migration/publications/migrationreport/ docs/MigrationReport2017_Highlights.pdf

United Nations, Department of Economic and Social Affairs, Population Division (2019): World Urbanization Prospects 2018 Highlights ST/ESA/ SER.A/421, New York: United Nations, p. 1. https://population.un.org/ wup/Publications/Files/WUP2018-Highlights.pdf

United Nations Development Programme (2009): Human Development Research Paper 2009/30 Cross-National Comparisons of Internal Migration, pp. 55. https://hdr.undp.org/system/files/documents/hdrp-200930pdf.pdf

Viviane, Clement/Kumari Rigaud, Kanta/de Sherbinin, Alex/Jones, Bryan/ Adamo, Susana/ Schewe, Jacob/Sadiq, Nian/Shabahat, Elham (2021): Groundswell Part 2: Acting on Internal Climate Migration. Washington, DC:The World Bank, p. xv. https://openknowledge.worldbank.org/handle/ 10986/36248

World Bank (2017): The Growing Role of Minerals and Metals for a Low Carbon Future, Washington: World Bank Publications, pp. 35. https:// documents1.worldbank.org/curated/en/207371500386458722/pdf/ 117581-WP-P159838-PUBLIC-ClimateSmartMiningJuly.pdf

World Bank (2021): Resilience COVID-19 Crisis Through a Migration Lens, Migration and Development Brief 34, Washington: World Bank Publications, p. 10. https://www.knomad.org/sites/default/files/2021-05/Migration%20and%20Development%20Brief%2034_1.pdf

World Bank (2022a): Annual Remittances Data (updated as of May 2021). https://www.worldbank.org/en/topic/migrationremittancesdiasporaissues/brief/migration-remittances-data

World Bank (2022b): A War in a Pandemic. Implications of the Ukraine crisis and COVID-19 on global governance of migration and remittance flows, Migration and Development Brief 36, Washington: World Bank Publications, p. 9. https://www.knomad.org/publication/migration-and-development-brief-36

Zahnd, A (2013): The Role of Renewable Energy Technology in Holistic Community Development, PhD thesis, Murdoch University, Perth. https:// www.springer.com/de/book/9783319039886

Der Nexus zwischen Klimawandel und menschlicher Mobilität und seine besondere Relevanz für urbane Räume

Benjamin Schraven

Die Folgen der globalen Erwärmung stellen die menschliche Sicherheit weltweit zunehmend vor große Herausforderungen. Dabei werden sowohl plötzlich einsetzende Ereignisse wie Stürme oder Flutwellen als auch eher schleichende Prozesse wie sich wandelnde Niederschlagscharakteristika zu immer größeren Bedrohungen für Ökosysteme sowie die Lebens- und Wirtschaftsgrundlagen von Millionen von Menschen (IPCC 2021). Gerade im globalen Norden zeigen sich viele Menschen besonders besorgt aufgrund der möglichen Auswirkungen dieser Gefahren auf die menschliche Mobilität. Seit Jahrzehnten werden von Politik und Medien Prognosen aufgegriffen, wonach der globale Norden mit zig Millionen „Klimaflüchtlingen" aus den von den Auswirkungen des Klimawandels besonders betroffenen Regionen des globalen Südens rechnen müsste (Schraven 2021). Andererseits rücken – auch aufgrund des weltweiten Urbanisierungstrends – die Themen Städte und Urbanisierung in den Fokus des Klimawandeldiskurses. Städte spielen auch eine entscheidende Rolle in (klimabezogenen) Mobilitätsmustern des globalen Südens, da die Auswirkungen des Klimawandels häufig bestehende Mobilitätsmuster verändern oder verstärken (z. B. bei der Land-Stadt-Migration; Roderick et al. 2021). Dieser Artikel setzt sich mit den Erkenntnissen der aktuellen Forschung zum Klimawandel-Mobilitäts-Nexus auseinander und skizziert deren Folgen und Herausforderungen für urbane Räume im globalen Süden. [1]

Klimawandel, menschliche Mobilität und die Stadt – Eine kurze Forschungsgeschichte

Die besondere Rolle von Städten im Kontext von Klima- und Umweltwandel ist schon lange Gegenstand der Forschung: Urbane Gebiete sind zum einen von den Folgen der Erderwärmung stark betroffen – dementsprechend stehen sie unter besonderem Anpassungsdruck – auf der anderen Seite kommt ihnen bei der Minderung von Treibhausgasemissionen ebenfalls eine besondere Rolle zu, da von ihnen ein Großteil der weltweiten Emissionen ausgeht (UNEP 2022). Auch die Migrationsbewegungen aus ländlichen Räumen in die Städte sind seit weit über 100 Jahren Gegenstand der Migrationsforschung (de Haas 2021). Interessanterweise spielten dagegen Klima- oder Umweltfaktoren in der Migrationsforschung lange eine allenfalls untergeordnete Rolle (Piguet 2013). Dies ändere sich erst langsam ab Mitte der 1980er Jahre, als das Umweltprogramm der Vereinten Nationen (UNEP) 1985 einen Bericht veröffentlichte, der auch die Definition des Begriffs „Umweltflüchtling" enthielt (El-Hinnawi 1985). Als „Umweltflüchtlinge" gelten nach dieser Definition diejenigen, die ihre angestammte Heimat verlassen müssen, weil Umweltereignisse dort ihre Existenz bedrohen. Diese Definition wird vielfach als zu vage abgelehnt. Die Veröffentlichung führte jedoch zu einer intensiven wissenschaftlichen Auseinandersetzung mit dem Thema (Schraven 2021).

Mit dieser aufkeimenden Diskussion in den späten 1980er und frühen 1990er Jahren konnten schnell zwei ziemlich unterschiedliche Lager in der wissenschaftlichen Gemeinschaft identifiziert werden, die die Debatte maßgeblich beeinflussten. Auf der einen Seite gab es die sogenannten „Alarmisten", die hauptsächlich Ökolog*innen, Klimawissenschaftler oder Biodiversitätsforscher waren. Ihre Analysen zum Zusammenhang zwischen Umweltveränderungen und menschlicher Mobilität basierten auf der Prä-

---

[1] Dieser Beitrag basiert u.a. auf einer vorangehenden englischsprachigen Publikation: „The Nexus between Climate Change and Human Mobility and its relevance for Urban Areas." (Schraven 2022).

misse, dass ökologische Veränderungen – und insbesondere die Folgen der globalen Erwärmung – eine zunehmend dominante Rolle bei Migrationsentscheidungen spielen würden. Eine weitere Grundannahme war, dass Umweltveränderungen menschliche Lebensräume zunehmend unbewohnbar machen – was immer mehr Menschen dazu bringen würde, ihre Heimat zu verlassen. Der bekannteste Vertreter der „Alarmisten" war Norman Myers, ein angesehener Experte auf dem Gebiet der Biodiversitätsforschung. In den 1990er Jahren veröffentlichte er eine Prognose, wonach es bis Mitte des 21. Jahrhunderts 200 Millionen „Klimaflüchtlinge" geben werde (Myers 1993). Diese Einschätzung sind in dieser Form schon lange nicht mehr haltbar und methodisch fragwürdig. Allerdings taucht diese Prognose bis in die 2020er Jahre hinein immer wieder in Medienberichten oder Äußerungen von Politikerinnen und Politikern zu den Folgen des Klimawandels auf. Andererseits beteiligte sich seit Anfang der 1990er Jahre eine bald als „Skeptiker" bezeichnete Gruppe von Wissenschaftlern an der wissenschaftlichen Debatte über den Zusammenhang zwischen Klimawandel und menschlicher Mobilität. Die Skeptiker kamen eher aus der Migrationsforschung, den Wirtschafts- oder Sozialwissenschaften. Ihre Sicht auf die Rolle ökologischer Faktoren war eine völlig andere als die der „Alarmisten". Sie gingen davon aus, dass Umwelteinflüsse nur einer von mehreren Faktoren sind, die menschliche Migrationsentscheidungen beeinflussen. Prognosen über die künftige Zahl von „Klimaflüchtlingen" lehnten sie ab – nicht zuletzt wegen der Schwierigkeit, zu definieren, wer unter eine solche Kategorie fällt (Brown 2008; Piguet 2013; Schraven 2021).

Die wissenschaftliche Debatte zum Klima-Migrations-Nexus basierte lange Zeit vor allem auf Einzelfallstudien. Dies änderte sich erst in den 2000er Jahren, als das öffentliche Interesse an dem Thema wuchs und internationale Organisationen wie die Internationale Organisation für Migration (IOM) oder das Flüchtlingshilfswerk der Vereinten Nationen (UNHCR) sich vermehrt mit der Problematik auseinandersetzten. Diese Situation hat seither die Etablierung zahlreicher internationaler Forschungsprojekte und -initiativen begünstigt, die sowohl den Fokus der bisherigen Forschung als auch die allgemeine Wissensbasis erheblich erweitert haben. Zu diesen Forschungsinitiativen zählen beispielsweise die Projekte „Environmental Change and Forced Migration Scenarios" (EACH-FOR), „Where the Rain Falls" oder „Migration, Environment and Climate Change: Evidence from Policy" (MECLEP) (Schraven 2021).

Klimawandel und menschliche Mobilität

Sicherlich gibt es noch einige Wissens- und Forschungslücken bezüglich des Zusammenhangs von Migration und Klimawandel. Die Ergebnisse der zum Teil oben aufgeführten Projekte und Initiativen lassen jedoch einige Rückschlüsse auf den (globalen) Zusammenhang zwischen Klimawandel und menschlicher Mobilität zu. Diese sollen, basierend auf einigen Meta-Analysen (Cattaneo et al. 2019; Hoffmann et al. 2020; Afifi et al. 2015; vgl. auch Schraven 2021), im Folgenden skizziert werden.

Die erhöhte Wahrscheinlichkeit plötzlich auftretender Gefahren wie Flutereignisse ist eine der deutlichen Folgen des Klimawandels. Millionen von Menschen sind dadurch in ihrer menschlichen Sicherheit bedroht. Darüber hinaus wirken sich langsam einsetzende Gefahren im Zusammenhang mit der globalen Erwärmung wie Änderungen von Niederschlagscharakteristika oder Küstenerosion zunehmend negativ auf die Nahrungsmittelproduktion, die Ernährungssicherheit oder die (traditionellen) Lebensgrundlagen aus. Dennoch bleiben auch angesichts dieser Umweltveränderungen menschliche Migrationsentscheidungen hochkomplex. Nicht nur die Folgen des Klimawandels führen dazu, dass Menschen ihren Wohnort verlassen. Vielmehr spielen viele Faktoren eine Rolle: Wirtschaftliche (z. B. Beschäftigungsperspektiven), politische (z. B. Visafreiheit) oder soziale Rahmenbedingungen (z. B. Zugang zu sozialen Netzwerken) können signifikant zur Entscheidung beitragen, ob jemand migriert oder nicht. Migrationsentscheidungen basieren meist nicht auf einer einzigen Ursache, sondern auf einem Zusammenspiel verschiedener Motive und Zwänge. So ist also nicht nur die Unterscheidung zwischen Flucht bzw. Zwangsmigration und freiwilliger Migration oft kaum zu leisten – gleiches gilt für die Unterscheidung zwischen Folgen des Klimawandels und nicht klimawandelbedingten Umweltereignissen als Faktoren der Migrationsentscheidung. Es ist äußerst schwierig festzustellen, ob ein bestimmter Migrationsprozess umwelt- oder klimabedingt ist oder ob man überhaupt etwa von „Klimamigration" sprechen sollte. Eine schlichte Ursache-Wirkung-Formel nach dem Motto „Je mehr Klimawandel, desto mehr Migration" lässt sich nicht aufstellen, zumal Migration offensichtlich nicht die einzige Reaktion auf die Folgen des Klimawandels ist. Es gibt grundsätzlich viele Möglichkeiten, sich „vor Ort" an veränderte Umgebungsbedingungen anzupassen. Beispielsweise können sich von Dürren betroffene Kleinbauern ihre landwirtschaftliche Produktion durch Wasserspeichertechnologien oder neue Anbautechniken an den Klimawandel anpassen und so an ihrem Herkunftsort bleiben.

Über das Ausmaß der bereits stattfindenden Zwangsmigration aufgrund von Katastrophen liegen Zahlen vor. So geht das Internal Displacement Monitoring Center (IDMC 2021) davon aus, dass im Jahr 2020 weltweit etwa 20 Millionen Menschen aufgrund von Katastrophen ihre Heimat verlassen mussten. Allerdings beinhalten diese Zahlen auch Migrationsbewegungen, bei denen die Betroffenen nach (sehr) kurzer Zeit an ihre Wohnorte zurückkehren. Daher sind sie – wie auch die gängigen Prognosen über die künftige Zahl der „Klimamigranten" im Allgemeinen – mit äußerster Vorsicht zu interpretieren.

Festzuhalten ist zudem, dass Menschen, die von den Auswirkungen des Klimawandels hauptsächlich betroffen sind – und für die Migration in diesem Zusammenhang eine Option sein kann oder gar muss – zum Großteil ärmeren Bevölkerungsgruppen des globalen Südens angehören. Es geht vor allem um kleinbäuerliche Familien, Viehnomaden oder urbane Arme. Aufgrund ihrer sehr begrenzten Ressourcenausstattung sind die allermeisten von ihnen nicht in der Lage, über weite Strecken zu migrieren. Klimabezogene Migration findet daher vor allem innerhalb von Ländern oder zwischen Nachbarländern (häufig in Form von zirkulärer Arbeitsmobilität) statt. Mit einem millionenfachen Ansturm von „Klimamigranten" in Richtung Europa ist daher auf absehbare Zeit nicht zu rechnen. Viele der Betroffenen sind gar so arm, dass sie nirgendwohin auswandern können und gewissermaßen in ihren Gehöften „gefangen" sind. In der Literatur werden sie teilweise als „trapped populations" (Government Office for Science 2011, S. 11) bezeichnet. Immobile oder immobilisierte Bevölkerungsgruppen sind und werden wahrscheinlich am stärksten von den Auswirkungen der globalen Erwärmung betroffen sein.

Wenn vom Klimawandel betroffenen Menschen jedoch in der Lage sind, sowohl mobil zu sein als auch etwas Geld zu verdienen, kann das verdiente Geld auch dazu beitragen, die Verluste bzw. Schäden zu kompensieren, die durch die Auswirkungen klimatischen Wandels verursacht wurden. Dementsprechend hat sich die Frage, ob und inwieweit Migration eine Risikominimierungs- oder gar Anpassungsstrategie an die negativen Auswirkungen des Klimawandels sein kann, zu einer der wichtigsten Fragestellungen in der Forschung zum Klima-Mobilitäts-Nexus in den letzten Jahren entwickelt. Da die Lebens- und Arbeitsbedingungen von Migranten im globalen Süden oft prekär sind, ist Migration als Bewältigungs- oder Anpassungsstrategie sicherlich kein „Selbstläufer". Zudem bedarf es noch einer tiefgreifenderen wissenschaftlichen und politischen Debatte, unter welchen Umständen von Migration als Bewältigungs- oder Anpassungsstrategie die Rede sein sollte. Einer allzu vereinfachenden Formel nach dem Motto „Migration bedeutet Anpassung" ist daher sehr skeptisch zu betrachten

„Klimamigration": Welche Rolle für die Städte?

Ganz offenkundig werden Städte weltweit und gerade auch in Ländern und Regionen des globalen Südens zu Wohnorten für immer mehr Menschen. Der Aufenthalt in den Städten ist jedoch oft nicht permanenter Natur. Ein wichtiges Ergebnis der Forschungsaktivitäten der letzten Jahre zum Klima-Mobilitäts-Nexus ist, dass Zirkularität ein herausragendes Merkmal (eher) freiwilliger Formen menschlicher Mobilität ist, die im Kontext des Klimawandels stattfinden (siehe oben). Zirkuläre Arbeitsmobilität, bei der einzelne Haushaltsmitglieder ihre Familie für eine begrenzte Zeit verlassen, um woanders zu leben und zu arbeiten, könnte in diesem Zusammenhang vielleicht als die ausgeprägteste Form menschlicher Mobilität angesehen werden – obwohl die Datenlage auch dazu keine genauen Zahlen hergibt, weder für die nationale noch für die globale Ebene. Auch wenn Begriffe wie „Landflucht" in etwas anderes vermuten lassen, ziehen ganze Haushalte eher selten in urbane Gebiete, und ländliche Gebiete werden in den kommenden Jahrzehnten höchstwahrscheinlich nicht einfach verschwinden. In Subsahara-Afrika zum Beispiel wird die absolute Zahl der Menschen, die in urbanen Gebieten leben, in den nächsten 20 bis 30 Jahren wahrscheinlich sogar noch zunehmen, und multilokale Haushaltsumgebungen sowie lebhafte Formen multilokalen Austausches (Geld, Wissen, materielle Güter usw.) zwischen ländlichen und urbanen Gebieten werden eher die Regel als die Ausnahme sein. Darüber hinaus wird urbanes Bevölkerungswachstum oft eher durch natürliches Bevölkerungswachstum in urbanen Gebieten und die Transformation vormals ländlicher Gebiete in das (peri-)urbanes Terrain angetrieben als durch Land-Stadt-Migration (Schraven 2016, Schraven 2022).

Darüber hinaus sind diese Migrationsströme sehr dynamisch: In Zeiten wirtschaftlicher Krisen oder politischer Instabilität – oder wie in den Jahren 2020 und 2021 aufgrund von weltweit umgesetzten Maßnahmen zur

Eindämmung der Ausbreitung von COVID-19-Pandemie – neigen viele in urbanen Gebieten lebende Migrant*innen (gendern) Migrierende oder Migrant*innen dazu, in ihre ländlichen Heimatorte zurückzukehren, um sich so zumindest rudimentär sozial abzusichern. Dementsprechend weisen in diesen Situationen manche Länder zeitweise sogar eine negative Land-Stadt-Wanderungsbilanz auf – mit anderen Worten: Die Migration aus den Städten in ländliche Räume übersteigt dann die Land-Stadt-Wanderungen (Lucas 2021).

Im Hinblick auf die Klimakrise sind Städte zunehmend mit den negativen Auswirkungen der globalen Erwärmung konfrontiert, was sich wiederum auf die Mobilität von und in die Städte auswirkt. Allein aufgrund des Anstiegs des Meeresspiegels ist davon auszugehen, dass zahlreiche Territorien (z. B. Teile der pazifischen Inselstaaten oder bestimmte Küstengebiete Bangladeschs) in den nächsten Jahrzehnten unbewohnbar werden mit der Konsequenz, dass viele Menschen langfristig diese Gebiete verlassen bzw. Regierungen Umsiedlungsmaßnahmen planen müssen. Das wird auch urbane Gebiete stark betreffen. Nicht nur mehr als die Hälfte der Weltbevölkerung lebt in Städten, sondern auch die meisten Gebäude und wirtschaftlichen Aktivitäten der Welt konzentrieren sich auf urbane Umgebungen. Viele Menschen und Wirtschaftszweige, die am anfälligsten für die Auswirkungen des Klimawandels sind, sind auch in urbanen Gebieten zu finden. Neben dem Anstieg des Meeresspiegels, steigenden Temperaturen und Hitzestress werden Sturmfluten, die Versauerung der Ozeane, Stürme oder Überschwemmungen entlang von Flüssen den Anteil von Stadtbewohnern, die Klimarisiken ausgesetzt sind, auf der ganzen Welt stark erhöhen. Informelle Siedlungen – in denen oft auch viele Migranten leben – sind besonders anfällig für die Folgen des Klimawandels und gerade durch extreme Wetterereignisse stark bedroht (IPCC 2021; 2014).

Daher ist es wahrscheinlich, dass viele Migrierende in Städten auf der ganzen Welt – und dies ist bereits heute der Fall, insbesondere in vielen hochwassergefährdeten Stadtgebieten – „Vom Regen in die Traufe"-Situationen erleben werden: Migrierende und Geflüchtete werden ihre vom Klimawandel betroffenen Heimstätten auf der Suche nach Schutz und (besseren) wirtschaftlichen Möglichkeiten verlassen und in Städten ebenso klima- bzw. umweltbedingte Risiken vorfinden. Umso dringlicher wird die Anpassung an den Klimawandel in urbanen Gebieten. Wenn diese Minderungs- oder Anpassungsmaßnahmen jedoch nicht erfolgreich umgesetzt werden, könnten mobile Bevölkerungen in ökologisch noch anfälligere Situationen geraten, was sich so wiederum auch auf multilokale Haushalte sehr negativ auswirken würde (siehe auch Roderick et al. 2021: 8).

Ausblick

Forschungsergebnisse zum Klima-Mobilitäts-Nexus komme zum Schluss, dass die Zusammenhänge zwischen Klimawandel und menschlicher Mobilität sehr komplexer Natur sind. In Bezug auf urbane Gebiete und Land-Stadt-Beziehungen stellt der Klimawandel nicht nur eine Bedrohung für ländliche und urbane Infrastrukturen aller Art dar. Er beeinträchtigt auch die Dynamik der Mobilitätsmuster zwischen Land und Stadt und der damit verbundenen translokalen Mechanismen. Hinsichtlich der politischen Herausforderungen von Klimawandel und menschlicher Mobilität im Kontext urbaner Gebiete betont der Mayor Migration Council (MMC) (Roderick et al. 2021) zum Schluss, dass es unerlässlich sein wird, a) urbane Akteure besser in internationale und nationale Entscheidungsstrukturen einzubinden, b) einen besseren Zugang zu finanziellen und technischen Ressourcen für urbane Akteure zu bekommen; und c) in diesem Zusammenhang stärkere und besser koordinierte politische Rahmenbedingungen für die Bewältigung der enormen Herausforderungen der Zukunft zu schaffen. In einem ersten Schritt ist es jedoch wichtig, städtischen Entscheidungsträgern, Experten und Praktikern ein klareres Verständnis der komplexen Dynamik von Klimawandel und Migration zu vermitteln und die besondere Rolle der Städte aufzuzeigen. Dies muss eine höhere Priorität bekommen – ansonsten wird das Ringen um politische Lösungen in diesem Kontext zunehmend schwieriger, wenn nicht gar aussichtsloser.

Literatur

Afifi, Tamer/Milan, Andrea/Etzold, Benjamin/Schraven, Benjamin/Rademacher-Schulz, Christina/Sakdapolrak, Patrick/Reif, Alexander/van der Geest, Kees /Warner, Koko (2015): "Human mobility in response to rainfall variability: opportunities for migration as a successful adaptation strategy in eight case studies.", in: Migration and Development 5/2. https://doi.org/10.1080/21632324.2015.1022974

Brown, Oliver (2008): "The numbers game.", in: Forced Migration Review 31, pp. 8–9.

Cattaneo, Cristina/Beine, Michel/Fröhlich, Christiane/Kniveton, Dominic/Martinez-Zarzoso, Inmaculada/Mastrorillo, Marina/Millock, Katrin/Piguet, Etienne/Schraven, Benjamin (2019): "Human Migration in the Era of Climate Change.", in: Review of Environmental Economics and Policy 13/2, pp. 189–206.

de Haas, Hein (2021): "A theory of migration: the aspirations-capabilities framework", in: Comparative Migration Studies 9, https://doi.org/10.1186/s40878-020-00210-4

El-Hinnawi, Essem (1985): Environmental refugees, Nairobi: United Nations Environment Programme.

Government Office for Science (2011): Foresight: Migration and Global Environmental Change. Final Project Report. London.

Hoffmann, Roman/Dimitrova, Anna/Muttarak, Raya/Crespo Cuaresma, Jesus/Peisker Jonas (2020): "A meta-analysis of country-level studies on environmental change and migration." in: Nature Climate Change 10, pp. 904–912.

Internal Displacement Monitoring Centre (IDMC) (2021): Global Report on Internal Displacement, Geneva: IDMC.

Intergovernmental Panel on Climate Change (IPCC) (2014): Climate Change 2014: Synthesis Report. Contribution of Working Groups I, II and III to the Fifth Assessment Report of the Intergovernmental Panel on Climate Change, Geneva: IPCC.

Intergovernmental Panel on Climate Change (IPCC) (2021): Synthesis report of the sixth assessment report: A report of the Intergovernmental Panel On Climate Change, Geneva: IPCC.

Lucas, Robert (2021): Crossing the Divide: Rural to Urban Migration in Developing Countries, Oxford: Oxford University Press.

Myers, Norman (1993). "Environmental refugees in a global warmed world", in: Bioscience 43(11), pp. 752-761.

Piguet, Etienne (2013): "From 'primitive migration' to 'climate refugees': The curious fate of the natural environment in migration studies.", in: Annals of the Association of American Geographers 10/1, pp. 148–162.

Roderick, William/Garg, Snigdha/Morel, Luisa Miranda/Brick, Kate/Powers, Maggie (2021): Cities, Climate and Migration: The role of cities at the climate-migration nexus, New York: C40/Mayors Migration Council.

Schraven, Benjamin (2022): „The Nexus between Climate Change and Human Mobility and its relevance for Urban Areas.", in: Trialog 140/141, pp. 10–12.

Schraven, Benjamin (2021): "'Die Klimaflüchtlinge kommen" – Über die Problematik einer Begrifflichkeit.", in: Leviathan 49/2, pp. 244–257.

Schraven, Benjamin (2016): "Migration dynamics in Sub-Saharan Africa – Myths, facts and challenges." In: Rural 21 50/2, pp. 27–29.

United Nations Environment Programme (UNEP) (2022): Cities and Climate Change. Nairobi: UNEP, https://www.unep.org/explore-topics/resource-efficiency/what-we-do/cities/cities-and-climate-change

Climate Change Games –
Dem Klimawandel spielerisch be- und entgegnen
Ein methodisch-strategischer Zugang
für eine kooperative Klimabildung

Horst Kanzian, Ingrid Huber

Dürren, Starkregenereignisse, Waldbrände, Meeresspiegelanstiege und Klimamigration sind nur einige Folgen des anthropogenen, d.h. vom Menschen verursachten, Klimawandels. Aufgrund der weitreichenden und z.T. dramatischen Auswirkungen sind vielfältige sowie gezielte Maßnahmen zum Klimaschutz und zur Klimawandelanpassung erforderlich. Besonders Schulen sind dazu aufgefordert, Klimabildung zu forcieren, um dieses Phänomen in seiner Komplexität zu verstehen, aber auch um die zukünftigen Generationen auf die zu erwartenden ökologischen, gesellschaftlichen sowie wirtschaftlichen Folgen des Klimawandels vorzubereiten. Für Pädagog*innen stellt sich in diesem Zusammenhang häufig die Frage, welche pädagogisch-didaktische Strategie oder welche Unterrichtsmethode in diesem relativ neuen Aktionsfeld besonders bildungs- und handlungswirksam ist. Im Folgenden soll ein Zugang vorgestellt werden, der auf einer Bildungskooperation fußt und sich den Spieltrieb des Menschen zu Nutze macht. In Form eines kooperativen Lernfeld-Projekts, in dem Schüler*innen unter Lernbegleitung von Studierenden gemeinsam ein Projekt umsetzen, wurden sog. Climate Change Games erstellt, die jeweils ein Stück weit eine Facette des Klimawandels beleuchten. Um Praktiker*innen und engagierten Multiplikator*innen einen Einblick zu geben, sollen in diesem Beitrag die theoretischen Hintergründe, das Umsetzungssetting sowie die (Lern-)Erfahrungen vorgestellt werden.

Klimabildung in Zeiten des Klimawandels

Der anthropogene Klimawandel, der mit Extrem(wetter)ereignissen wie
Dürren, Überflutungen, Hitzewellen, schmelzenden Gletschern und einem
stetig ansteigenden Meeresspiegel einhergeht, hat weitreichende Auswirkungen auf viele gesellschaftliche Bereiche und zählt deshalb zu den
größten Herausforderungen in diesem Jahrhundert (Heinrichs/Grunen-
berg 2009: 14–15). Um das Phänomen des Klimawandels und dessen Risiken
und Folgen einzudämmen, ist vielseitiges sowie integratives Handeln un-
umgänglich. Im Mittelpunkt der Diskussionen rund um den Klimawandel
stehen somit Maßnahmen zum Klimaschutz, die wiederum gesellschaftliche Aufklärungs- und Bildungsarbeit erfordern. Schulen sind in diesem
Zusammenhang wichtige Instanzen, da Kinder und Jugendliche hinsichtlich Klimaschutz und -anpassung als zentrale Akteure „für die notwendige
und bevorstehende soziale, ökonomische und ökologische Transformation"
(Trautmann/Siegmund 2021: 296) gelten. Für Pädagog*innen in Schulen
erwächst daraus die besondere Verantwortung, Klimabildung und -erzie-
hung zu forcieren, damit nachhaltiges Klimahandeln resultiert. Das von
der UNESCO bereits 2010 forcierte Programm zur Klimabildung (Climate
Change Education for Sustainable Development) ist ein Teilbereich der Bildung für nachhaltige Entwicklung (BNE), die wiederum als Schlüsselelement
zur Erreichung aller 17 Sustainable Development Goals (SDGs) der Vereinten
Nation gilt (UNESCO 2021: 14; HMUKLV 2022: 5). Ziel der Klimabildung ist
es, sowohl Kenntnisse als auch ein Bewusstsein für die Ursachen, Dynamik
und Folgen des Klimawandels und entsprechende Bewältigungsstrategien
zu vermitteln bzw. zu entwickeln (Trautmann/Siegmund 2021: 296). Dadurch können die Lernenden den Klimawandel in den Wesenszügen (besser)
verstehen, klimawirksame Entscheidungen treffen und passende Maßnahmen zum Klimaschutz ergreifen (HMUKLV 2022: 5). Mittel- oder langfristig
soll es gelingen, eine hinsichtlich der Folgen des Klimawandels kompetente
und gleichzeitig resiliente Gesellschaft und Wirtschaft aufzubauen, zumal
– so viel ist sicher – uns dieses Phänomen noch länger beschäftigen wird
(Trautmann/Siegmund 2021: 296). Die Frage ist, mit welchen Strategien und
methodischen Zugängen diese Klimabildung realisiert werden kann bzw.
sollte, damit die Bildungswirksamkeit hoch ausfällt bzw. eine nachhaltige
Bildungsarbeit resultiert? Dieses Thema nur im Frontalunterricht aufzu-
arbeiten, ist angesichts lerntheoretischer Annahmen und der Komplexität

des Themas wenig erfolgversprechend. Es bedarf daher Zugänge, die auf den Erfahrungen der Schüler*innen aufbauen, möglichst ungezwungen wirken, Spaß machen, die Kreativität ankurbeln und dennoch Kompetenzen im Sinne der Klimabildung erweitern. Was nach einer pädagogisch-didaktischen Wundertüte klingt, könnte mit Klimaspielen und Spielen zum Klimaschutz erreicht werden, die aus der Feder bzw. dem Gedankengut der Schüler*innen entspringen.

Climate Change Games – Der Klimawandel ist kein Spiel – oder doch?!

Spiele sind zwar in der Alltagskommunikation in aller Munde, basieren jedoch aufgrund der Theorievielfalt auf keiner allgemein anerkannten Definition (Bernhardt 2018: 13). Vielmehr existieren eine Reihe von Merkmalseigenschaften, die listenartig den Spielbegriff ausdeuten. Demnach werden (Gesellschafts-)Spiele oft als zweckfreie, handlungsorientierte und prozesshafte Aktivitäten umschrieben, die in (lockerer) Gesellschaft zum Vergnügen ausgetragen werden und der Erreichung eines regelbasierten Ziels in einer Scheinwelt dienen (Rinschede/Siegmund 2020: 261). Im Unterricht eingesetzte Spiele lehnen sich an diese allgemeinen Merkmale an und erfüllen zudem pädagogisch-didaktische Prinzipen. In diesem Kontext sind Spiele Unterrichtsmethoden bzw. Lernformen, die „offenes, handlungsorientiertes ‚Arbeiten‘" (ebd.: 261) ermöglichen. Es wird diesen Unterrichtsspielen daher keine (völlige) Zweckfreiheit unterstellt, sondern das besondere Potenzial des Spielens für das Lernen betont. Spiele werden in diesem Sinne instrumentalisiert und dienen u.a. der Erreichung bestimmter Kompetenzen wie z.B. der Sach-, Methoden-, Moral- und Sozialkompetenz (Bernhardt 2018: 27; Rinschede/Siegmund 2020: 261). Aus diesem Grund werden im Unterricht häufig Lernspiele eingesetzt, die die „Verfolgung überprüfbarer Lernziele vorsehen" (Bernhardt 2018: 57) und neben der Vermittlung von Fachwissen der spielerischen Festigung von Kenntnissen sowie Fertigkeiten dienen. An die Regeln und äußere Form von Gesellschaftsspielen angelehnt, kommen hierbei u.a. Brett-, Karten-, Quartett-, Puzzle-, Rate-, Quiz-, Memory- und Tabu-Spiele zum Einsatz, die im Allgemeinen eine intensive Auseinandersetzung mit den Lerngegenständen und (damit) einen erhöhten Lernerfolg versprechen (Rinschede/Siegmund 2020: 261–262).

Climate Change Games, also Spiele zum Klimawandel und Klimaschutz, sind im Verständnis der beiden Autor*innen spezielle Lernspiele, die im Unterricht eingesetzt werden, um Schüler*innen die Grundlagen, Ursachen, Zusammenhänge und Auswirkungen des Klimawandels sowie mögliche Handlungsmöglichkeiten im Sinne des Klimaschutzes spielerisch zu vermitteln bzw. zu festigen. Die Spiele, die digital, analog oder hybrid sein können, erweitern somit das Wissen und das Bewusstsein rund um das Phänomen des Klimas und des Klimawandels, thematisieren Herausforderungen, Probleme und Lösungen und eignen sich daher besonders dazu, Klimabildung im Unterricht zu realisieren; und zwar auf eine lustbetonte, regelbasierte und benotungsfreie Art und Weise (Rinschede/Siegmund 2020: 262). Gerade bei diesem komplexen und weitreichenden Thema sind Spiele besonders gut geeignet, um das vernetzte Wissen sowie Denken zu fördern und „Zusammenhänge, Abhängigkeiten sowie raumbezogene Prozesse" (ebd.: 262) verständlich(er) zu vermitteln. Dabei machen sich Climate Change Games mehr als andere Spiele die Symbolfähigkeit zu Nutze, also dem Potenzial des Spiels, die „Welt modellhaft abzubilden und diese dem Unterrichtsprozess damit zugänglich zu machen" (Bernhardt 2018: 32). Gerade ein globales Thema, wie es der Klimawandel ist, kann auf diese Weise einfacher dargestellt und begreifbarer gemacht werden. Besonders lernwirksam ist – v.a. bei digitalen Spielen – die Möglichkeit der spielerischen Simulation von Klimaphänomenen, deren Leistung darin besteht, „in zeitlich geraffter und didaktisch reduzierter Form komplexe historische oder gegenwärtige Prozesse, die für die Jugendlichen real nicht erlebbar sind, im Spiel erlebbar zu machen" (Sitte 2001: 81). Folgen des Meeresspiegelanstiegs, Dürren und das Abschmelzen von Polkappen können derart relativ einfach und unkompliziert nachgeahmt werden. Bestenfalls können die spielbasierten Lernformen dazu beitragen, dass sich das positive Verhalten in der Modell- bzw. Scheinwelt auf die reale Welt überträgt und das Handeln hinsichtlich Klimaschutz entsprechend verändert. Gut konzipierte Klimaspiele und Spiele zum Klimaschutz gehen also über das Unterhaltsame hinaus und inhärieren das Potenzial, „einen Beitrag zur Bewältigung von Klimaherausforderungen" (Gerber et al. 2021: 2, übersetzt) zu leisten. Das rückt die Climate Change Games in die Nähe von Serious Games, die neben der Unterhaltung der spielerischen Vermittlung und Aufarbeitung von ernsten Themen dient.

Climate Change Games im Unterricht für Klimabildung heranzuziehen ist eine pädagogisch-didaktische Strategie, die seit den Fridays-for-Future-

Bewegungen an Bedeutung gewonnen hat. Hierzu gibt es mittlerweile einige (Kopier-)Vorlagen und Best-Practice-Beispiele, die es Pädagog*innen erleichtern, diese speziellen Lernspiele mit wenig Vorbereitungsaufwand direkt im Unterricht einzusetzen (siehe u.a. Gehenzig 2016). Wesentlich herausfordernder sind Zugänge, die auf den Spielerfahrungen der Lerner*innen aufbauen, und Klimaspiele als Lernoutput entstehen lassen. In diesem Zusammenhang agieren die Schüler*innen in der Rolle als Spielentwickler*innen und benötigen neben dem Sachverständnis auch basales Konzeptions- und Konstruktionswissen für die Erstellung dieser Spiele. Im engeren Sinne müssen die Schüler*innen sich im Klaren werden, welche Spielform angestrebt wird und wie hierzu der Spielmechanismus, der Spielinhalt und die Gestaltung des Spiels aussehen sollen. Während also der Spielinhalt die Scheinwelt bzw. die Story ausmacht, in die das Spiel eingebettet ist, regelt der Spielmechanismus den Spielablauf und versteht sich als Motor des Spiels. Die optische Präsentation sowie die für das Spielen erforderliche Ausstattung (u.a. Spielanleitung, -utensilien) sind wiederum Gestaltungsentscheidungen, die besonders kreative Leistungen erfordern (Uhlenwinkel 2013: 66). Da für die Spielerfindung und -erstellung umfassende Arbeiten anfallen und unterschiedlichste Fertigkeiten benötigt werden, ist ein größeres Lernunternehmen notwendig. Für die Umsetzung wurde daher auf das „kooperative Lernfeld-Projekt" (Huber/Kanzian 2022: 149) zurückgegriffen, das im Folgenden kurz vorgestellt werden soll.

Umsetzungssetting

Die Climate Change Games wurden im Schuljahr 2020/21 im Zuge eines kooperativen Lernfeld-Projekts realisiert, das ein Alleinstellungsmerkmal in der Lehramtsausbildung in der Sekundarstufe am Standort der Universität Klagenfurt ist. Dabei handelt es sich um eine institutionsübergreifende Form der Projektarbeit, bei der Schüler*innen mit Lernunterstützung durch Lehramtsstudierenden ein Projekt zu einem (aktuellen) geographischen, schulstandort- oder schulschwerpunktspezifischen Thema umsetzen. Im Fall der erwähnten Spiele wurde das Projekt mit 23 Schüler*innen der 9. Schulstufe des Ingeborg-Bachmann-Gymnasiums in Klagenfurt (Kooperationsschule der Universität Klagenfurt) und ebenso vielen Lehramtsstudierenden erstellt. Während die Lerner*innen der involvierten Klasse ein echtes

Projekt im Unterrichtsfach Geographie und wirtschaftliche Bildung umsetzen und dabei i.d.R. mit zeitgemäßen Themen, Methoden sowie Medien in Kontakt kommen, fungieren die Student*innen als Lernbegleiter*innen und können die an der Universität thematisierte Projektmethode praktisch erproben. Dabei durchlaufen die Lernenden in Kleingruppen zu je max. 5 Schüler*innen die Projektphasen nach Frey (2012) und können nach einem Semester an Projektarbeit auf wertvolle Ergebnisse, i.d.F. Climate Change Games, blicken. In diesem Kontext entstehen viele Praxis- und Projekterfahrungen sowie Synergieeffekte, von denen alle Beteiligten profitieren.

Projektergebnisse

Die folgende Tabelle (Tab. 1) gibt einen Überblick über die entstandenen Climate-Change-Games, die im Lernfeld-Projekt im Zuge der Projektarbeit entstanden sind und im Jahr 2021 mit dem Energy Globe Award Austria (Kategorie: Jugend) prämiert wurden. Sie gelten als Unikate, da sie – entgegen professionellen Spielen – aus der Kreativität bzw. aus der Feder der Schüler*innen entsprungen sind (siehe Beispiel „Waldivit", Abb. 1). In ihrer Rolle als Spielentwickler*innen hat man bei Schüler*innen gut beobachten können, welche Themen ihnen beim Klimaschutz wichtig sind und welche Facetten dieser komplexen, integrativen sowie weitreichenden Materie sie besonders affizieren. Die Ergebnisse zeigen, dass sich die Jugendlichen zwar an bekannte Lernspielformen anlehnten, diese aber z.T. geschickt mit neuen Aspekten verknüpften und dadurch interessante Spielemechanismen hervorbrachten. Dadurch resultierten innovative Spielvarianten wie z.B. das Klima-Memory mit integrierten QR-Codes. Letztere können mit der Smartphone-Kamera gescannt werden und leiten anschließend auf die App „Actionbound" (Actionbound GmbH 2022: o.S.) weiter, die das digitale Beantworten von selbst definierten Fragen zum Thema ermöglicht. In diesem Zusammenhang kamen mitunter auch hybride Spiele zustande, die analoge und digitale Elemente innerhalb eines Klimaspiels vereinten. Diese Zugänge spiegeln den Zeitgeist der aktuellen Spielelandschaft wider und lassen zudem erkennen, was den Schüler*innen bei dieser besonderen Spieleform wichtig ist. Auf diese Weise ist viel implizites Wissen zur Spielekonzeption entstanden, das für professionelle Spielehersteller, die junge Menschen für dieses Thema sensibilisieren wollen, wie auch für Pädagog*innen interessant sein könnte. Aus diesem Grund sollen im Folgenden die wichtigsten Lernerfahrungen dargestellt werden.

Tabelle 1: Tabellarische Übersicht zu den Climate Change Games

Name Thema Spielform	Kurzbeschreibung zum Climate-Change-Game
Waldivit Waldbrände Activity	Die Spieler*innen müssen verschiedene Begriffe mit verschiedenen Schwierigkeitsgraden zum Thema Waldbrände zeichnen und/oder erklären.
Natural Disasters Memory Naturkatastrophen Memory-Quiz	Die Spieler*innen müssen Kärtchen richtig aufdecken und dabei – fallweise – Fragen zum Thema Naturkatastrophen beantworten.
Klima-Memory Regionale Produkte Memory mit QR-Codes	Auf den Memory-Karten befinden sich QR-Codes, die mit dem Smartphone gescannt werden und zu weiterführenden Fragen in der App „Actionbound" führen, die die Spieler*innen digital beantworten müssen.
Sea Level Meeresspiegelanstieg Memory	Klassisches Memory-Spiel, das das Thema „Meeresspiegelanstieg" aufgreift. Ziel des Spiels ist es, möglichst viele Kartenpärchen zu finden.
Eisbär und Pinguin Schmelzende Polkappen Brettspiel	Ziel dieses Spieles ist es, so viele Fragen wie möglich richtig zu beantworten, um so viele Tiere (Eisbären oder Pinguine) wie möglich vor dem Aussterben zu retten.
Das CO2-Monster Lebensmitteltransporte Brettspiel mit Quizelementen	Die Spieler*innen müssen leichte, mittelschwere und schwierige Fragen zur Thematik beantworten und dürfen – nach richtiger Beantwortung – mit der Spielfigur ein Feld weiterziehen.
Knacknüsse der Mülltrennung Mülltrennung Zuordnungsspiel	In diesem digitalen Spiel werden die Knacknüsse der Mülltrennung aufgegriffen und damit die Mülltrennung gefestigt.

Quelle: Eigene Darstellung.

Abbildung 1: Klimaspiel „Waldivit" mit dem Themenschwerpunkt Waldbrände (Quelle: Eigene Aufnahme)

(Lern-)Erfahrungen

Nach erfolgreicher Umsetzung wurde das Projekt an beiden Institutionen mittels schriftlicher Reflexionen und Feedbackgesprächen evaluiert. Ziel war es, ein differenziertes qualitatives Bild zu diesem strategischen Zugang von den direkt Beteiligten zu erhalten, um diese Erfahrungen mit anderen Pädagog*innen, die als Multiplikatoren agieren wollen, zu teilen.

Die Auswertung der schriftlichen Reflexionen ergab, dass die Schüler*innen über alle Arbeitsgruppen hinweg sehr positiv resümieren und es gut fanden, dass sie das Projekt in Kooperation mit den Studierenden umsetzen konnten. Obwohl es in jeder Gruppe zwar „Höhen und Tiefen" (R1 2021: 1), „meist lange Arbeitszeiten" (R8 2021: 1) sowie Phasen gab, in denen man das „Arbeiten als eher mühsam empfand" (R12 2021: 1), war es insgesamt für viele Lernenden eine „großartige" (R6 2021: 1), „interessante und lehrreiche Erfahrung" (R10 2021: 1), die mit Spaß einherging. Die Schüler*innen begrüßten den Zugang, „ein eigenes Spiel zu entwickeln und zu designen" (R8 2021: 1) und waren auf das Ergebnis letztlich „sehr stolz" (R2 2021: 1). Aufgrund der positiven Rückmeldungen schaut man mit einem „Lächeln darauf zurück" (R3 2021: 1) und „würde das Projekt wieder machen" (R6 2021: 1). Die insgesamt äußerst positiven Rückmeldungen zeigen, dass die Lernenden motivationale Erfahrungen gemacht und auf kommunikative bzw. interaktive Weise sich einem globalen Problem auf handelnde sowie kreative Weise genähert haben.

Die Studierenden empfanden die Projektarbeit mit den Schülerinnen und Schülern aufgrund der digitalen Austragung als sehr anstrengend und (technisch) herausfordernd, aber als sehr lehrreich, da sie die Projektmethode nach der theoretischen Behandlung gleich praktisch mit einer Schulklasse ausprobieren konnten. Wichtig empfanden sie, dass die Schüler*innen gut in das Thema eingeführt werden, bevor das Projekt beginnt, um entsprechend darauf aufbauen zu können. Ebenso erachteten sie es für bedeutsam, dass die Spielideen nicht ‚aufgedrückt' werden, da damit die Kreativität gehemmt und die Motivation der Schüler*innen im Projektunterricht wesentlich sinkt.

Aus der Sicht der Fachlehrerin wurde angemerkt, dass durch die projektbasierte Beschäftigung ein Thema behandelt wurde, zu dem die Schüler*innen aufgrund von z.B. regionalen Naturkatastrophen bereits direkten Kontakt hatten und das deshalb für einige einen sehr ernsten Charakter mit sich bringt. Dementsprechend wurde mit der Entwicklung von Climate Change Games ein Zugang eröffnet, um ein (fallweise) negatives oder mit Zukunftsängsten behaftetes Thema mit einem lockeren Lernzugang positiv zu konnotieren. Den Klimaspielen können also lernpsychologische Effekte zugesprochen werden, die im Detail noch näher hinterfragt werden müssten. Ferner wurde positiv hervorgehoben, dass bei diesem Projekt interessensgeleitet eine Facette des weitreichenden Phänomens eingehend vertieft und dabei Präkonzepte zum Klimawandel entsprechend erweitert bzw. korrigiert wurden. Allenfalls ist daher empfehlenswert, entsprechende Reflexionsphasen nach dem Spiel einzuplanen, um die Spielerfahrungen mit den Schüler*innen zu besprechen. Durch die gegenseitigen Spiele-Erprobungen konnte der Klimawandel über alle Gruppen hinweg besser nachvollzogen und die Auswirkungen, wie bspw. Klimamigration eine ist, eingehend(er) rekapituliert werden. Dadurch konnten mit den spielerischen Zugängen das vernetzte Denken gefördert und die Weichen für anknüpfbares Wissen gelegt werden. Offen bleibt, inwiefern bzw. wie sehr diese aus der Sicht der Lehrkraft doch zeitaufwändigen Zugänge eine Verhaltensänderung hinsichtlich des Klimaschutzes bewirken und die Handlungen im Sinne der Klimawandelanpassung nachhaltig beeinflussen konnten. Wenn auch in diesem Punkt noch weitere Forschungen notwendig sind, so haben Feedbackgespräche mit Schüler*innen eine insgesamt sehr nachhaltige Wirkung erahnen lassen. So konnte festgestellt werden, dass die selbst erstellen Spiele zum Anlass genommen wurden, um in Zeiten der Lockdowns zu Hause einen Spieleabend im Familienkreis zu veranstalten. Durch diese Rückmeldung ist anzunehmen, dass die Effekte des Projekts weitreichender sind als zu Beginn angenommen und die erstellten Spiele als multiplikative Medien fungieren. Dadurch wird informelles Lernen initiiert, wovon Jung und Alt – wie auf Spielen oft propagiert – profitieren. Wie daraus abzuleiten ist, haben diese speziellen Lernspiele also nicht nur eine schulische, sondern auch eine außerschulische Wirkung und reißen andere hinsichtlich der Klimabildung mit in den Bann.

Zusammenfassung und Ausblick

Der anthropogene Klimawandel hat weitreichende Auswirkungen auf viele gesellschaftliche Bereiche und zählt deshalb zu den größten Herausforderungen des 21. Jahrhunderts. Um das Phänomen des Klimawandels sowie dessen Risiken und Folgen einzudämmen, ist vielseitiges Handeln erforderlich. Für Pädagog*innen in Schulen erwächst daraus die besondere Verantwortung, Klimabildung und -erziehung zu forcieren, damit nachhaltiges Klimahandeln resultiert. Das erfordert effiziente und nachhaltige Strategien, um bei den Schüler*innen eine hohe Lernwirksamkeit zu erzielen. Eine Möglichkeit Klimabildung umzusetzen, ist die projektbasierte Erstellung von Climate Change Games als Lernprodukte. Sie gelten im Sinne der beiden Autor*innen als spezielle Lernspiele und sollen die Grundlagen, Ursachen, Zusammenhänge und Auswirkungen des Klimawandels sowie diverse Handlungsmöglichkeiten im Sinne des Klimaschutzes spielerisch vermitteln bzw. festigen. Als Umsetzungssetting empfiehlt sich das institutionsübergreifende Konzept des kooperativen Lernfeld-Projekts, da die Erstellung dieser Lernprodukte durchaus viel Zeit, Betreuung und vielfältige lernseitige Kompetenzen erfordern. Die Evaluierung hat gezeigt, dass die Schüler*innen in der Rolle als Spieleentwickler*innen diesen Zugang zwar als aufwendig und anstrengend, aber auch als sehr interessant und lehrreich empfinden. Eine Gelingensbedingung ist jedoch, dass sie im Sinne der offenen Lernform möglichst frei agieren und die Spiele nach eigenen Vorstellungen erstellen können; anderenfalls führt dies zu demotivierenden Erfahrungen und Kreativitätsverlusten. Offen bleibt, inwiefern diese speziellen Spiele das Handeln hinsichtlich Klimawandel und -schutz beeinflussen. Entsprechende Rückmeldungen der Schüler*innen, die diese Spiele auch im Familienverband ausprobierten, lassen jedoch hinter Climate Change Games starke multiplikative Wirkungen vermuten.

Literatur

Actionbound GmbH (2022): Actionbound. https://de.actionbound.com/ vom 28.07.2022.

Bernhardt, Markus (2018): Das Spiel im Geschichtsunterricht, Frankfurt am Main: Wochenschau-Verlag.

Frey, Karl (2012): Die Projektmethode (12. Auflage), Weinheim und Basel: Beltz-Verlag.

Gehenzig, Melanie (2016): Klimaspiele. Unkomplizierte Methoden für die Bildungsarbeit. Bonn: Germanwatch. https://www.germanwatch.org/de/13445 vom 29.07.2022.

Gerber, Andreas/Ulrich, Markus/Wäger, Flurin X./Roca-Puigròs, Marta/Gonçalves, João S. V./Wäger, Patrick (2021): "Games on Climate Change: Identifying Development Potentials through Advanced Classification and Game Characteristics Mapping", in: Sustainability 13 (4), S. 1–26.

Heinrichs, Harald/Grunenberg, Heiko (2009): Klimawandel und Gesellschaft. Perspektive Adaptionskommunikation (1. Auflage), Wiesbaden: VS Verlag für Sozialwissenschaften, GWV Fachverlage GmbH.

Hessisches Ministerium für Umwelt, Klimaschutz, Landwirtschaft und Verbraucherschutz (HMUKLV) (2022): Qualitätsrahmen Klimabildung. Handreichung für Lehrende im Bereich Klimabildung für nachhaltige Entwicklung. https://www.klimabildung-hessen.de/files/content/Klima%20%26%20Bildung/Qualit%C3%A4tsentwicklung/Qualita%CC%88tsrahmen%20Klimabildung.pdf vom 01.08.2022.

Huber, Ingrid/Kanzian, Horst (2022): „Kooperative Lernfeld-Projekte im Geographie- und Wirtschaftskundeunterricht. Chancen, Synergieeffekte und Herausforderungen für die geographiedidaktische Hochschullehre und die involvierte Schule", in: Markus Pissarek/Martin Wieser/Judith Koren/Vesna Kucher/Verena Novak-Geiger (Hg.), Projektbezogene Kooperation von Schule und Universität. Synergien, Gelingensbedingungen, Evaluation, Münster und New York: Waxmann, S. 149–170.

Reflexion (R) 1, 2, 3, 6, 8, 10, 12 (2021): Reflexion zur Durchführung des Lernfeld-Projekts zum Thema Climate Change Games: Dem Klimawandel spielerisch begegnen, Klagenfurt: Ingeborg-Bachmann-Gymnasium.

Rinschede, Gisbert/Siegmund, Alexander (2020): Geographiedidaktik (4. Auflage), Paderborn: Ferdinand Schöningh.

Sitte, Wolfgang (2001): „Didaktische Spiele", in: Wolfgang Sitte/Helmut Wohlschlägl (Hg.), Beiträge zur Didaktik des Geographie und Wirtschaftskunde-Unterrichts, Wien: Institut für Geographie und Regionalforschung, S. 76–89.

Trautmann, Christina/Siegmund, Alexander (2021): „Förderung der Handlungsfähigkeit von Auszubildenden für die betriebliche Klimaanpassung", in: Standort 45, S. 294–301.

Uhlenwinkel, Anke (2013): „Spiele im Geographieunterricht", in: Manfred Rolfes/Anke Uhlenwinkel (Hg.), Essays zur Didaktik der Geographie. Schriftenreihe: Potsdamer Geographische Praxis 6, Potsdam: Universitätsverlag, S. 63–70.

UNESCO (2010): The UNESCO Climate Change Initiative. Climate Change Cducation for Custainable Cevelopment. https://unesdoc.unesco.org/ark:/48223/pf0000190101/PDF/190101eng.pdf.multi vom 05.08.2022.

UNESCO (2021): Bildung für nachhaltige Entwicklung. Eine Roadmap. https://www.unesco.de/sites/default/files/2021-10/BNE_2030_Roadmap_DE_web-PDF_nicht-bf.pdf vom 06.08.2022.

The Micropolitics of Climate-Related Planned Relocation in the Maldives
A Case for Multiple Im/mobility Pathways

Brooke Wilmsen, Fazeela Ibrahim

Introduction

According to the Intergovernmental Panel on Climate Change (IPCC 2022), responses to ongoing sea level rise and land subsistence in low-lying coastal settlements and small islands include protection, accommodation, and planned relocation (also called planned retreat or government organised resettlement). Protection and accommodation are generally considered in situ adaptation responses as they do not require migration (Tan/Liu/Hugo 2016) and support voluntary immobility (Yee/Piggott-McKellar/McMichael/McNamara 2022). In contrast, planned relocation is an ex situ response that can be voluntary and/or involuntary (see Wilmsen/Webber 2015 for discussion). It is generally considered inevitable that some form of planned relocation will be required in response to climate change (Gussmann/Hinkel 2020), particularly for small island developing states.

Although in situ adaptation generally carries a lower risk of maladaptation[1] for a range of socio-cultural, political, psychological, and affective reasons, planned relocation is gaining momentum over other responses (Farbotko/Dun/Thornton/McNamara/McMichael 2020). This is despite scholars advising that planned relocation should be a last resort response to climate change due to its high risk of maladaptation (Wilmsen/Webber 2015, Sid-

---

1 Maladaptation is defined as an intervention in one location or sector that could increase the vulnerability of another location or sector or increase the vulnerability of the target group to future climate change (Nobel/Huq/Anokhin/Carmin 2014).

ers/Ajibade 2021, See/Wilmsen 2020, Rogers/Xue 2015, Barnett/O'Neill 2012, Farbotko/Dun/Thornton/McNamara/McMichael 2020). However, even though climate-related planned relocation is underway in the Philippines (See/Wilmsen 2020), Fiji (Pill 2020) and the Maldives (Kothari 2015), there are limited studies on which to base this assertion.

Evidence that planned relocation could be maladaptive is mostly drawn from other contexts—poverty alleviation, environmental protection, urban expansion, and infrastructure development. Planned relocation in these contexts suggests it ruptures the social fabric of communities and produces abrupt and intergenerational impoverishment (Rogers/Wang 2006, Quetulio-navarra/Niehof/Vaart/Horst 2012, Downing 1996, Cernea 1997). Whilst such studies are helpful for understanding the impacts of climate-related planned relocation, there is urgent need to gather evidence in places where it is already occurring.

Owing to its topography and low elevation (average of 1.5 metres above sea level), the Maldives is one of the most vulnerable countries to climate change[2]. The dispersal of the population across 187 small and remote islands, creates diseconomies of scale and high transport costs, challenging government responses to climate change. Due to regional weather patterns, inundation, coastal erosion, and disasters such as tsunamis are the key impacts of climate change in the Maldives (United Nations 2005). It is estimated that under extreme projections of sea level rise, 85% could be underwater by the year 2100 (Sovacool 2012: 296). However, even small changes in sea level could mean extensive land inundation (ADB 2021) and our research suggests this is already occurring. Catalysed by the 2004 tsunami, the Maldives is one of the first countries in the world to implement climate-related planned relocation. Yet, beyond the work of Kothari (2014) and Gussmann/Hinkel (2020), it has hardly been studied. This research fills this gap by exploring a planned relocation in the Maldives after the 2004 tsunami.

---

2 The Maldives was described by former president Nasheed in his speech to the United Nations as the climate change "canary in the coal mine" (Hirsch 2015: 190).

2004 Tsunami in the Maldives

The 2004 tsunami was a critical event in the Maldives' climate history. It struck on December 26th, killing 83 residents. Although the death rate was low relative to other countries, around one-third of the population on 39 Maldivian islands was impacted. Damage was estimated at around 470 million USD (United Nations 2005), with 10 percent of houses suffering damage and around 20,000 people displaced (Pardasani 2006). The environmental impacts were also extensive, including, erosion and ground water contamination (Pardasani 2006). The southern atolls of Meemu, Thaa and Laamu were most severely impacted (Rasheed/Warder/Plancherel/Piggott 2022). Of the 34 deaths on Meemu atoll, 16 were on Kolhufushi, and around 346 buildings were reportedly lost or damaged (Fritz 2006).

The central government responded to the tsunami by intensifying planned relocation. Drawing on the 1997 Population Consolidation Policy (PCP) and 2001 'National Population Consolidation Strategy and Programme', the Gayoom government planned to consolidate the population in two regional growth centres and on 85 islands (Gussmann/Hinkel 2020, Kothari 2014). The aim was to increase economies of scale, service delivery, living standards and economic opportunities (Gussmann/Hinkel 2020). While early attempts at relocation, for example, at Hithadhoo, were met with resistance, the tsunami provided an opportunity to reframe the programme around reducing coastal risk (Gussmann/Hinkel 2020, Kothari 2014). Of the 17 communities the government planned to relocate, 14 were finally resettled (Gussmann/Hinkel 2020).

To understand the lived experience of planned relocation after the tsunami, we selected one of the most badly impacted islands on Meemu. Rather than planned relocation to another island, planned relocation at Kolhufushi was within the island. Other contexts suggest that small scale relocations, over short distances, where communities relocate together and maintain access to livelihood resources have the best chance of long-term success. Thus, unlike island-to-island resettlement, planned relocation on Kolhufushi was at least theoretically more likely to succeed. Even so, before we began our fieldwork, we became aware of significant issues on Kolhufushi. Still, we felt this provided an opportunity to understand the complexities of the lived experience of planned relocation.

Although we planned to conduct fieldwork at the resettlement, on arrival at Kolhufushi in December 2021 it was clear that not everyone had relocated. Some households had repaired their pre-tsunami homes in the northern and southern settlements. As such we modified our sampling strategy to capture these households (in situ management/voluntary immobility) and those who moved to new homes in the resettlement (planned relocation/ex situ response/mobility). With the assistance of the island council, we selected households in the northern and southern in situ sites and in the central resettlement. We also spoke to a range of women (seven) and men (six) of different ages (37–77 years old). In total, 13 interviews were conducted (10 respondents from the community, two former island executives, and current island council members). Interviews were conducted in Dhivehi and later translated and transcribed into English. In what follows, we present our findings by unpacking the micropolitics on Kolhufushi which was the dominant theme framing their lived experiences of planned relocation.

The Micropolitics of Planned Relocation

Although the political divisions that emerged on Kolhufushi dominated interviewees' narratives, in the initial days and months after the tsunami they emphasised community unity. The first two weeks after the tsunami were spent in the island school, followed by six months in tents before moving into temporary shelters close to the harbour. Invariably this period is described as a time when the residents banded together to respond to the devastation:

> "Even for about one year after the tsunami ...or till around five or six months, everyone stayed together. Till then, all of us were extremely close, we cooked and ate together" (Mahmood[3], male, 43 years, planned relocation).

However, as the period in the temporary shelters stretched from months into years, tolerances for extreme heat, overcrowding, limited privacy, and inadequate toilet facilities waned. In desperation, some people decided to return to their damaged houses:

---

3 All names have been changed to pseudonyms.

"It was extremely difficult to live in temporary shelters because I also have my parents, my husband, my siblings who are also married, three unmarried men and three unmarried women so they couldn't sleep in the same room. We are married couples so they couldn't also sleep in our rooms and so we moved back home" (Hafsa, female, 45 years, in situ management).

On observing the return of some residents to their pre-tsunami homes and following a central government directive, the executive of Kolhufushi insisted that households remain in the temporary shelters where provisions such as food relief, water and electricity would only be provided. This stoked animosities in the community:

"After we moved back to our house … we were denied the basic necessities and stones were thrown at our house at night" (Hafsa, female, 45 years, in situ management).

The rigidity of the central government's response to the tsunami extended to its planned relocation, exacerbating the growing divisions in the community. Regardless of former land size, lost and damaged houses would be replaced with new houses on 3000 m² plots in the resettlement. While this suited most households, the poorest and the richest were disadvantaged. In the case of the former, those who held land before the tsunami but had been unable to afford to build a house were ineligible for new housing. In the case of the latter, those who held plots between 7000 and 20,000 m² before the tsunami were expected to move to a 3000 m² plot in the resettlement like the other residents. These families tended to be the most powerful on the island, the most vocal, the most resistant and as such, turned several other families against the planned relocation:

"One of the influential people was a relative of the housing minister who had four plots of around 20,000 sq ft [sic] which they had to let go and this led to a lot of problems." (Former island executive of Kolhufushi).

In 2005, the Red Cross, contracted by the Maumoon government to build the resettlement, arrived at Kolhufushi to construct the first 50 houses. As the central government had promised survivors "a house for a house", the residents were expecting at least 250 houses to be built and were extremely upset about the plan:

> "After keeping the residents in such poor conditions for that long, it was disappointing that they would build only 50 houses and they said if they are to build houses they need to build houses for all the residents" (current island council officials).

In late 2005, central government representatives came to Kolhufushi to negotiate, but the residents occupied the harbour and refused to let them disembark. The island executive was called to the capital to explain why they were not fulfilling their responsibilities as the government's representatives on the island. The island executives were in a difficult position—caught between the imposed resettlement and social unrest on Kolhufushi:

> "I was taken by the government and asked why I am against its decisions. I said the residents are only expressing their anger. They thought it was because of me but no it was because they had promised more houses, but now they are only constructing 50 houses. I said its okay if they think I'm responsible. Then they released me. When I returned, the residents closed the office and I officially resigned".

The deadlock continued until President Nasheed won the first direct presidential elections in 2008. Although generally regarded as a period of instability, it heralded greater freedoms for Maldivians. Island chiefs were replaced by democratically elected island councils headed by a president and vice-president. The new island council of Kolhufushi was aligned with President Nasheed, which helped to break the stalemate on Kolhufushi. In 2010 the Nasheed government allowed the residents of Kolhufushi to self-determine their path to reconstruction:

> "Since the presidency changed, those who wanted houses built on their own land are building them or if they want housing under the plan (resettlement site) they can" (Salma, female, 40 years, planned relocation).

In 2012, after almost a decade of conflict, unbearable living conditions and associated trauma, the households finally moved into permanent replacement housing. Interviewees generally expressed satisfaction with this housing; however, climate related issues remain, suggesting maladaptation:

> "The difficulties we face are worse now. You can see that the saltwater reaches to the back of my house. The island is eroded, the beautiful mangrove river area is almost gone, and many leaders have said they'd do something, but they're still stuck surveying. The water tastes good while it rains, but it smells bad when there's no rain" (Nazim, male, 61 years, planned relocation).

The protracted conflict on Kolhufushi had long lasting impacts. One of the main themes of our interviews was community disarticulation. People spoke about the children "no longer playing together", thatching being undertaken within private houses "rather than as a communal activity on the beach" and the general "coldness" within the community. Hasna (female, 54 years, planned relocation) describes the situation,

> "At least in my heart, I feel like there's a big distance between us. Because in the past, even though we weren't blood related, it felt like we were; now it feels so distant. The atmosphere now feels very unfriendly and inhospitable. It's not the same".

Although the election of Nasheed helped to progress reconstruction on Kolhufushi, it added a macro political element to the fissures in the community. Residents' alliances were split along national political lines, the MDP (Maldivian Democratic Party) and the PPM (Progressive Party of the Maldives), resulting in an escalation of the existing unrest on the island. According to our interviewees, infrastructure built by the island council (aligned with the MDP) was regularly destroyed by those who supported the PPM. Children were even caught up in the conflict, sent to push political propaganda and take part in the destruction. This has had profound impacts on relationships on the island with people noting:

> "But what really ruined relationships was the silly political dramas and ploys. With the new political wave, people's relationships got strained and they became difficult" (Mahmood, male, 43 years, planned relocation).

Im/mobility preferences

The protracted situation on Kolhufushi can in part be attributed to the central government's staunch commitment to planned relocation after the tsunami. By ignoring the preferences of powerful residents to retain their land and repair their houses, the government stoked political division that led to ongoing social disarticulation and ten years of unbearable living conditions. Whilst the powerful on the island loudly articulated their preference to remain in situ, other interviewees revealed other preferences:

> "If they consulted me, I would've gone to Gan Island (Laamu Attoll); an island big enough and developed enough that there are many ways to earn a living" (Nazim, male, 61 years, planned relocation).

Others would have moved closer to the capital:

> "I would prefer to live on an island my heart desired, and if I had a choice, I'd choose islands closer to Malé, the capital" (Ahmed, male, 68 years, planned relocation).

And,

> "If my husband gets a plot of land on Hulhumalé I would go" (Seema, female, 37 years, planned relocation).

Finally, some people preferred planned relocation to another island.

> "If we were on another island the government officials would treat everybody the same. If that was the plan, I would have moved. I'm fine with that being on any island in any atoll" (Hafsa, female, 45 years, in situ management).

The former island executives of Kolhufushi revealed that soon after the tsunami there were discussions with the central government about relocating the population of Kolhufushi to another island. Since relocation was politically controversial and generally unpopular, this option was never proposed to the residents and was rejected by the island leadership in favour of resettlement to the centre of the island. This decision demonstrates that the government presumed to know what was in the best interest of the residents. However, had it listened to the residents and provided support for multiple mobility and immobility pathways, perhaps conflict could have been avoided.

Discussion and Conclusion: Multiple Im/mobility Pathways

That planned relocation rarely follows a linear trajectory is not a new finding. Literature in other contexts is thick with studies of government organised resettlements that did not go to plan (Mathur 2006, Nguyen/Lobry de bruyn/ Koech 2016, Smyth/Esteves/Franks/Vaz 2015, Vanclay 2017, Wilmsen 2019); nor, is it novel to observe climate-related planned relocation as political. The politics of climate change adaptation is emerging as a key concern for researchers (See/Wilmsen 2020, Funder/ Mweemba/Nyambe 2018, Eriksen/ Nightingale/Eakin 2015). Some see politics as a condition that supports or derails the expectations attached to adaptation interventions (Few/Morchain/Spear/Mensah/Bendapudi 2017). Others conceptualise "adaptation as politics" because it inherently speaks to issues of power, conflicting policy preferences, resource allocation and administrative tensions (Dolšak/ Prakash 2018). Whereas others point out that the political contestation observed is often not about climate or even adaptation but instead about who accesses resources, who is authorised to govern and who is considered worthy of assistance (Nightingale 2017). Indeed, planned relocation at Kolhufushi laid bare the messy micropolitics of the island as elites struggled to retain control over their resources.

While our research adds another troubled case of planned relocation to the emerging register, our interviews also demonstrate the diverse mobility preferences of a small number of residents within one small island community in responding to an extreme weather event—in situ reconstruction, within island resettlement, relocation to another island and migration. Yet, the central government never consulted the residents, instead imposing planned relocation and leaving the island leadership to deal with the fallout. It's rigid commitment to planned relocation precluded other more locally relevant and socially acceptable mobility responses. This reiterates findings elsewhere that in attempting to tightly control mobility, planned relocation blinds governments to diverse, community driven responses (See/McKinnon/Wilmsen 2022). At Kolhufushi this resulted in conflict and a decade of unbearable living conditions that undermined the long-term cohesiveness of Kolhufushi. One interviewee summed up the disconnect between the government and local people:

> "They are not the ones living here. They live in their royal palaces, while we are the ones who live one day on the reef, the next day on the sea, and the other day we're planting trees, to earn our living. They cannot grasp our lifestyle, our situation" (Khalid, male, 60 years, in situ management).

Depending on their socio-economic positioning, resources and power, island residents have diverse preferences for where they live, how they rebuild after an extreme weather event and how they anticipate withstanding future climate events. This research supports the contention of Barnett and O'Neill (2012) and Yee et al. (2022) that to be successful and sustainable, adaptation strategies must acknowledge resources, needs, perspectives, preferences, and values of local people. Whilst our findings reaffirm the central role of acknowledging local knowledges and im/mobility preferences in producing socially acceptable responses to extreme weather events, we extend on previous research by highlighting the heterogeneous nature of its considerations. Even within one small community there can be multiple im/mobility pathways, and these should be supported so far as social cohesion can be maintained.

References

Barnett, Jon/O'Neill, Saffron J. (2012): "Islands, resettlement and adaptation", in: Nature Climate Change, 2, p. 8–10.

Cernea, Michael (1997): "The risks and reconstruction model for resettling displaced populations", in: World Development, 25, p. 1569–1587.

Dolšak, Nives/Prakash, Aseem (2018): "The politics of climate change adaptation", in: Annual Review of Environment and Resources, 43, S. 317–341.

Downing, Theodore E. (1996): Mitigating social impoverishment when people are displaced, in: Christopher, McDowell, (ed.) Understanding impoverishment: the consequences of development-induced displacement. Providence & Oxford: Berghahn Books, p. 33–48.

Eriksen, Siri. H./Nightingale, Andrea. J./Eakin, Hallie (2015): "Reframing adaptation: the political nature of climate change adaptation", in: Global Environmental Change, 35, p. 523–533.

Farbotko, Carol/Dun, Olivia/Thornton, Fanny/McNamara, Karen/McMichael, Celia (2020): "Relocation planning must address voluntary immobility", in: Nature Climate Change, 10, p. 702–704.

Few, Roger/Morchain, Daniel/Spear, Dian/Mensah, Adelina/Bendapudi, Ramkumar (2017): "Transformation, adaptation and development: relating concepts to practice", in: Palgrave Communications, 3, p. 17092.

Fritz, Hermann. M./Synolakis, Costas E./McAdoo, Brian G. (2006): "Maldives field survey after the december 2004 indian ocean tsunami", in: Earthquake Spectra, 22, p. 137–154.

Funder, Mikkel/Mweemba, Carol/Nyambe, Imasiku (2018): "The politics of climate change adaptation in development: authority, resource control and state intervention in rural zambia.", in: The Journal of Development Studies, 54, p. 30–46.

Gussmann, Geronimo/Hinkel, Jochen (2020): "What drives relocation policies in the maldives?", in: Climatic Change, 163, p. 931–951.

Hirsch, Eric (2015): " 'It won't be any good to have democracy if we don't have a country': climate change and the politics of synecdoche in the maldives.", in: Global Environmental Change, 35, p. 190–198.

IPCC (2022): "Summary for policymakers", in: Hans-Otto Pörtner (eds.), Climate change 2022: impacts, adaptation and vulnerability. Contribution of working group ii to the sixth assessment report of the intergovernmental panel on climate change. Cambridge University Press: Cambridge.

Kothari, Uma (2014): "Political discourses of climate change and migration: resettlement policies in the maldives: political discourses of climate change and migration.", in: The Geographical Journal, 180, p. 130–140.

Mathur, Hari Mohan (2006): Resettling people displaced by development projects: some critical management issues. Social Change, 36, p. 36–86.

Nguyen, Hien Thanh/Lobry de Bruyn, Lisa/Koech, Richard (2016): "Impact of hydropower dam development on agriculturally based livelihoods of resettled communities: a case study of Duong Hoa Commune in Central Vietnam", in: International Journal of Water Resources Development, 32, p. 978–996.

Nightingale, Andrea J. (2017): "Power and politics in climate change adaptation efforts: Struggles over authority and recognition in the context of political instability", in: Geoforum, 84, p. 11–20.

Ian R. Noble/Huq, Saleemul/Anokhin, Yuri A./Carmin, Jo Ann/Goudou, Dieudonne/Lansigan, Felino P. /Osman-Elasha, Balgis/Villamizar, Alicia/ Patt, Anthony/Takeuchi, Kuniyoshi/Chu, Eric (2014): "Adaptation needs and options", in: Climate Change 2014: Impacts, Adaptation and Vulnerability. Contribution of Working Group II to the Fifth Assessment Report of the Intergovernmental Panel on Climate Change, Ch. 14. Cambridge University Press: Cambridge

Pardasani, Manoj (2006): "Tsunami reconstruction and redevelopment in the maldives: a case study of community participation and social action", in: Disaster Prevention and Management, 15, p. 79–91.

Pill, Melanie (2020): "Planned relocation from the impacts of climate change in small island developing states: the intersection between adaptation and loss and damage", in: Leal F. Walter, (ed.) Managing climate change adaptation in the pacific region. Springer International Publishing: Cham, p. 129–149.

Quetulio-navarra, Melissa/Niehof, Anke/van der Vaart, Wander (2012): "The disruption and rebuilding of social capital in involuntary resettlement in the philippines and indonesia", in: International Journal of Social Sciences and Humanity Studies, 4, p. 307–323.

Rasheed, Shuaib/Warder,Simon C./Plancherel, Yves/Piggott, Matthew D. (2022): "Nearshore tsunami amplitudes across the maldives archipelago due to worst case seismic scenarios in the indian ocean", in: Natural Hazards Earth System Sciences, p. 1–27.

Rogers, Sarah/Wang, Mark (2006): "Environmental resettlement and social dis/re-articulation in Inner Mongolia, China", in: Population and Environment, 28, p. 41–68.

Rogers, Sarah/Xue, Tao (2015): "Resettlement and climate change vulnerability: evidence from rural china", in: Global Environmental Change, 35, p. 62–69.

Sovacool, Benjamin K. (2012): "Expert views of climate change adaptation in the Maldives", in: Climatic Change, 114, p. 295–300.

See, Justin/McKinnon, Katharine/Wilmsen, Brooke (2022): "Diverse pathways to climate change adaptation through a post-development lens: the case of Tambaliza island, Philippines", in: Climate and Development, p. 1–12.

See, Justin/Wilmsen, Brooke (2020): "Just adaptation? Generating new vulnerabilities and shaping adaptive capacities through the politics of climate-related resettlement in a Philippine coastal city", in: Global Environmental Change, 65, p. 102188.

Siders, A.R./Ajibade, Idowu (2021): "Introduction: managed retreat and environmental justice in a changing climate", in: Journal of Environmental Studies and Sciences, 11, p. 287–293.

Smyth, Eddie/Steyn, Michael/Esteves, Ana Maria/Franks, Daniel M./Vaz, Kemal (2015): "Five 'big' issues for land access, resettlement and livelihood restoration practice: findings of an international symposium", in: Impact Assessment and Project Appraisal, 33, p. 220–225.

Tan, Yan/Liu, Xuchun/Hugo, Graeme (2016): "Exploring the relationship between social inequality and envionmentally-induced migration: evidence from urban households in Shanghai and Nanjing of China", in: Robert McLeman/Jeanette Schade/Thomas Faist (eds.), Environmental migration and social inequality. Springer: Cham, p. 73–90.

United Nations (2005): Tsunami: impact and recovery—joint needs assessment. Reliefweb.

Vanclay, Frank (2017): "Project-induced displacement and resettlement: from impoverishment risks to an opportunity for development?", in: Impact Assessment and Project Appraisal, 35, p. 3–21.

Wilmsen, Brooke/Adjartey, David/Hulten, Andrew van (2019): Challenging the risks-based model of involuntary resettlement using evidence from the Bui dam, Ghana. International Journal of Water Resources Development, 35, p. 682–700.

Wilmsen, Brooke/Wang, Mark (2015): "Voluntary and involuntary reset-
    tlement in China: a false dichotomy?", in: Development in Practice, 25,
    p. 612–627.
Wilmsen, Brooke/Webber, Michael (2015): What can we learn from the prac-
    tice of development-forced displacement and resettlement for organised
    resettlements in response to climate change?", in: Geoforum, 58, p. 76–
    85.
Yee, Merewalesi/Piggott-Mckellar, Annah E./McMichael, Celia/ McNamara,
    Karen E. (2022): "Climate change, voluntary immobility, and place-be-
    longingness: insights from Togoru, Fiji", in: Climate, 10(3), S. 46.

Building Climate Resilience Through Migration in Thailand

Patrick Sakdapolrak, Harald Sterly[1]

Thailand is particularly vulnerable to droughts and floods. The country has experienced a number of extreme-weather events in recent years, including severe flooding in 2011 that inundated Bangkok and large tracts of central Thailand for weeks, as well as an extended period of drought in 2015–2016 that was the worst seen in decades.

These types of events affect the country as a whole, but rural, agrarian communities in the poor and dry Northeast region can be considered particularly lacking in resilience to environmental changes. There is little evidence to date that climate or environmental factors clearly and directly prompt migration, however environmental and especially climate risks play important roles in destabilizing rural agricultural livelihoods. These risks, in turn, increase the likelihood for some household members to migrate, as it becomes increasingly difficult for them to earn a living. This is a significant consideration, given that about 30 percent of the Thai workforce is employed in an agricultural sector dominated by small-scale family farms. But instead of merely an escape route, migration can also be a way for households to proactively guard themselves against increasing effects of climate change on local environments and livelihoods.

---

1   This article was originally published by the Migration Information Source, the online journal of the Migration Policy Institute, in December 2020. It is available online at: https://www.migrationpolicy.org/article/building-climate-resilience-through-migration-thailand

Worldwide, migration amid environmental change is today discussed primarily in the context of crises, conflicts, and humanitarian disasters, and is considered to be something negative that should be prevented. The phenomenon is framed as a sign of failed adaptation, with the migrants themselves usually portrayed as passive victims. This narrative is often adopted by the media, politicians, and practitioners who claim as many as 1.5 billion people could be forced to migrate by 2050 due to climate change.

However, the conversation is largely decoupled from state-of-the-art social science findings. There is widespread agreement in academia that these apocalyptic numbers of future "climate refugees" lack sound methodological and empirical basis, and must be regarded as guesstimates at best. There is also a lack of recognition that migration itself, whether internal or international, can be a successful adaptation. Furthermore, migration is a normal part of life for many people, with an estimated 272 million international migrants and more than 760 million internal migrants worldwide as of 2019. Environmental change, therefore, always occurs within a broader context of populations already migrating for one reason or another.

The crucial question, then, is under what circumstances does migration have the potential to generate positive effects for coping with and adapting to environmental change? This article, partly based on a 2019 policy brief for the German Federal Agency for Civic Education, offers perspectives from Thailand. It analyzes interactions between environmental change and migration and offers the notion of "translocal resilience" as a useful framework for evaluating ways that individuals, households, and communities can employ migration to offset some of the hazards of a changing environment.

Success or Failure: The Many Facets of Mobility and Immobility in the Context of Climate Change

While environmental factors certainly influence peoples' livelihoods and their decisions to migrate, migration in turn also influences how those exposed to climatic and environmental risks are able to cope with and adapt to them.

The case of Pom is illustrative. At age 19, he left his village in Northeast Thailand and moved to Singapore to find work. During 21 years there, he rose from construction worker to foreman, sending the equivalent of 1,500 euros per month to his family in Thailand. Pom used the money to buy additional land in Thailand and, upon return, also relied on the business acumen he had developed abroad to realize various commercial ventures there, including a pig farm and a karaoke bar.

Pom's decision to migrate turned out to be a profitable one for him and his family, and it cut against the prevailing and longstanding perception of migration amid environmental risk as a last resort for ailing communities.

The Complexity of Migration

Numerous empirical studies show there is no direct, monocausal connection between environmental or climate change and migration. Human mobility is extremely complex. The impact of environmental or climate change on migration is mediated through economic, social, and political processes. Migration should therefore be acknowledged as just one of the manifold livelihoods strategies households adopt to deal with stresses that emerge from environmental change.

Against this background, analysts' interpretation and assessment of mobility amid climate change can vary greatly. On the one hand, migration can be an indicator of a household or community's failure or inability to deal with risks. For example, a drought can lead to the complete collapse of an agricultural system, meaning that tried-and-tested coping strategies such as granaries and adaptation measures such as developing alternative local sources of income have failed. In this case, migration may be the last resort to ensure survival. On the other hand, as in Pom's case, migration can itself be a successful adaptation. In the onset of a drought situation, for instance, some households could send a member to work in the city; the urban worker then sends money back to the household to compensate for crop failures. In this case, migration would be successfully employed to manage a crisis.

It is important to note that not everyone who is affected by events such as droughts has to, wants to, or is able to migrate. Like migration, immobility cuts both ways. On the one hand, immobility can be a sign of great vulnerability and unsuccessful adaptation, such as when a household's in-situ coping mechanisms fail but people lack the necessary skills and resources to move. On the other hand, immobility can also be a sign of resilience, such as for households able to cope with the effects of environmental stresses locally, with available resources. These households do not need to be mobile in order to ensure their survival.

These explanations show that neither mobility nor immobility in the context of climate change can per se be interpreted as success or failure. Instead of framing migration as either a failure or success, it makes more sense to consider the degree of freedom that individuals and households have in their decision whether or not to migrate, in order to improve their livelihood situation or cope with or adapt to environmental change.

Conceptualizing the Contribution of Migration: From Migration as Adaptation to "Translocal Resilience"

The positive view of migration as a potentially successful way to deal with stress situations amid climate change has been increasingly recognized in academic and political debate, although this perspective receded somewhat following Europe's migration and refugee crisis of 2015–2016. To describe migration's potential in this context, the International Organization for Migration (IOM) uses the phrase „migration as adaptation." Analysis revolves primarily around the role of remittances, in the form of financial remittances as well as the transfer of knowledge and ideas, and is centered on managing, facilitating, and regulating migration in the context of risks. This discussion makes an important contribution to balancing the widespread but one-sided, negative view of migration in the context of climate change.

The notion of "translocal resilience" offers a conceptual framework that does more justice to the complexity of the nexus of migration and climate change. It observes that, regardless of expected climatic change, migration is a global social phenomenon and will continue to be an important driver and aspect of global change. Migration, in other words, is not something extraordinary that only occurs in crisis situations, but is already an integral part of the livelihoods of many people and households worldwide. A comprehensive understanding of the relationship between the environment and migration therefore requires a consideration of mobility, especially in the context of vulnerable livelihood systems. People's everyday vulnerability—not only that brought about by extreme situations or in response to extraordinary events—is of central importance.

Moreover, migration is not a process that begins with one's departure from her or her region of origin and ends with arrival somewhere else. Migration connects people, changes places, enables the permanent exchange of knowledge and resources, and thus creates a networked translocal social space. It intensifies the relationships between different places, in turn strengthening the ability of individuals and households to deal with climate-related risks and maintain or increase their wellbeing.

Translocal resilience can therefore be defined as the ability of individuals, households, and communities to uphold connections and navigate across distances in order to increase their ability to withstand shocks and hazards associated with climate and environmental change. A better understanding and, possibly, strengthening of this concept thus requires a focus on the interactions of the individuals, conditions, and connections that link migrants in places of destinations and households at places of origin, including social and economic elements. Considering the structures of these constellations and the agencies of individuals involved helps to reveal and understand conditions of translocal resilience.

Strengthening Resilience Through Translocal Relations: Practical Examples From Thailand

Resilience therefore depends on the constellation of characteristics of migrants at places of destination and households at places of origin, their multilevel embedding in social, economic, and other structures at the respective places, and the strength and dynamics of the relations and interactions between them. Examples from the authors' field research in Thailand illustrate qualities of translocal resilience, showing under which conditions migration can contribute to enhanced resilience against environmental risks.

As noted earlier, the authors could not find cases in Northeast Thailand in which migration could be directly attributed to climate factors. Yet the destabilization of agricultural livelihoods because of changing climate increases the likelihood of migration by some family members. Thus, regardless of the immediate drivers, rural migration—both to other parts of Thailand and internationally—and the ensuing connections between migrants and their origin households can help the households enhance resilience against current and future environmental risks.

Characteristics of migrants and their origin households, their embedding in community and larger structures, and their relations and interactions with each other can lead to dramatically different outcomes. However, the authors have noted some general patterns, among them that the socioeconomic status of the household at the place of origin is highly influential. It affects whether there are the resources for migration, either internationally or internally; the migrant's education and skills; and the household's dependence on regular remittances, which affects what demands the migrants perceive.

Precarity of migrants' place-of-origin household are thus often mirrored in working and living conditions at destination. Lamai, a 42-year-old female internal migrant who worked in a garment factory in Bangkok, came from a highly indebted, poor farming household that lacked income sources and depended on her remittances. Lamai also had to repay an informal, high-interest loan in the city that she took to pay down her family's debts. She could not afford to take risks to improve her and her family's situation and did not see any option other than continuing to make ends meet for both her urban and rural family. These kinds of situations tend to lead to stagnation and a "coping trap", instead of adaptations and improved livelihoods.

Inversely, the case of Phichit, a 40-year-old man who worked at a Bangkok factory, shows how better resource endowment paves the way for more positive development. Phichit came from a better-off rural farming household and finished secondary school before moving to Bangkok. As his household of origin did not need remittances, he could save enough to afford a bachelor's degree, which in turn enabled him to obtain a better paid and permanent position at the factory. He invested in his parents' farm, building ponds and acquiring livestock, and during visits helped villagers write funding proposals and development activities.

Social and Financial Remittances Combined

The density and quality of migrants' social relations depend on a range of factors, including generational and filial structures, gender relations, and the embedding and positionality at their places of destination. For Thai laborers migrating to Singapore, for example, exclusionary and segregationist policies at destination can contribute to them retaining a strong orientation towards families and rural origin villages in Thailand.

Translocal interactions between migrants and their households of origin are epitomized in different types of remittances. In addition to financial transfers that can help sustain household income and buffer against losses, migrants may transmit social remittances in the form of ideas, skills, innovations, and changed perceptions of risks and opportunities, which play an important role in households' resilience. Studying the experiences of these Thai migrants in Singapore, Simon Alexander Peth and Patrick Sakdapolrak show that a combination of financial and social remittances leads to transformation and changed practices, while financial remittances alone tend to maintain the status quo, and social remittances such as new ideas can often get "lost" without sufficient material support.

Pom, mentioned earlier in the article, represents one example of the successful strengthening of social resilience through a combination of financial and social remittances. The income and skills that he acquired through migration enabled him and his family to diversify their income base, making them less vulnerable to environmental and climatic risks.

However, in many cases migrants' working conditions are so different from their places of origin that their skills, knowledge, and ideas cannot easily be transferred. This was the case with Thong, a 29-year-old return migrant from Northeast Thailand who worked in industrialized farming in Israel for five years. The drip irrigation scheme he operated in Israel depended on sophisticated computer technology; even with all the necessary technical skills to set up such a system in Thailand, he simply could not afford the technology and hardware.

Implications for Policy

This analysis shows that migration can and does contribute to increased resilience that can be beneficial in the event that migrants' households are exposed to greater climate risks. The extent to which that is the case depends on a number of conditions and factors both at places of origin and destination, most of which offer entry points for policy action beyond traditional migration management. Among these factors are the socioeconomic situations of households of origin and migrants' ability to send financial remittances and gain knowledge, skills, and ideas to better cope with or adapt to risk. As one example of possible policy moves, rural and agricultural development organizations could offer investment training to households with migrants, remotely involve absentee migrants in local activities and community development strategies, or view return migrants as potential agents of change and offer appropriate financial or organizational support.

Whether migrants can send both financial and social remittances to a significant extent also depends on a range of policy areas. Migration policy certainly plays a role here, especially for international migration, as legal barriers drive the financial and organizational costs that can be decisive for an individual's ability to afford to migrate. But other policy fields are also highly relevant, shaping for example migrants' working conditions, payment and social insurance schemes, health care, housing conditions, and education for them and their children. It is important to also acknowledge the special vulnerabilities of migrants on their journey and often also in their destinations.

The debate on environmental migration should be re-centered from its current focus on national security and instead prioritize human security. It should aim to strengthen the capacity of those who are vulnerable to adapt and increase their freedom to decide whether to move or to stay. However, this seems difficult at present, given the polarization around migration in many places around the world. On the one hand, the environment-migration nexus has become a topic of concern in recent years and was mentioned in the United Nations-backed Global Compact for Safe, Orderly, and Regular Migration. On the other hand, the policy debate in a number of countries has been increasingly dominated by nationalistic sentiments. Together with COVID-19-related mobility restrictions, it remains an open question whether wealthy countries such as the United States or those in Europe would welcome immigrants to enhance resilience against climate risks.

In this light, a translocal resilience perspective could contribute to a more nuanced view of the nexus of environmental change and migration. Through the multiple entry points for policy that translocal resilience opens up, it broadens the options for policymakers to concretely support migration as a strategy of adaptation.

Migration not as Failure to Adapt, but Part of Adaptation

Climate change already is increasingly threatening human security, especially among vulnerable populations in the global South. Mobility patterns are being influenced and changed. However, the relationship between environmental change and migration is more complex and multilayered than simple representations suggest. Migration in this context should not be seen only as the result of a household's failure to adapt, but can also be part and parcel of the process of successful adaptation.

Apart from simply better managing migration and instead of deterring it, as many countries have prioritized, there is room to improve migrants' situations and instead of deterring it, as many countries have prioritized, there is room to improve migrants' situations and enhance their ability to contribute to climate resilience for themselves and their families. Doing so means going beyond managing migration to better managing translocality.

References

Ayeb-Karlsson, Sonja/Smith, Christopher D./Kniveton, Dominic (2018): "A Discursive Review of the Textual Use of 'Trapped' in Environmental Migration Studies: The Conceptual Birth and Troubled Teenage Years of Trapped Populations", in: Ambio 47: 557–573. https://doi.org/10.1007/s13280-017-1007-6

Bell, Martin/Charles-Edwards, Elin (2013): Cross-National Comparisons of Internal Migration: An Update on Global Patterns and Trends. Technical Paper No. 2013/01, United Nations Department of Economic and Social Affairs, New York. https://www.un.org/en/development/desa/population/publications/pdf/technical/TP2013-1.pdf

Bettini, Giovanni (2013): "Climate Barbarians at the Gate? A Critique of Apocalyptic Narratives on 'Climate Refugees.' ", in: Geoforum, 45, p. 63–72. https://doi.org/10.1016/j.geoforum.2012.09.009

Black, Richard, W./Adger, Neil/Arnell, Nigel W./Dercon, Stefan/Geddes, Andrew et al. (2011): "The Effect of Environmental Change on Human Migration", in: Global Environmental Change, 21(1), pp. 3–11. https://doi.org/10.1016/j.gloenvcha.2011.10.001

Borderon, Marion/Sakdapolrak, Patrick/Muttarak, Raya/Kebede, Endale/ Pagogna, Raffaella et al. (2019): "Migration Influenced by Environmental Change in Africa: A Systematic Review of Empirical Evidence", Demographic Research, 41, p. 491–544. https://doi.org/10.4054/DemRes. 2019.41.18

Etzold, Benjamin/Sakdapolrak, Patrick (2012): "Globale Arbeit – lokale Verwundbarkeit: Internationale Arbeitsmigration in der geographischen Verwundbarkeitsforschung.", in: Migration und Entwicklung aus geographischer Perspektive, ed. by Malte Steinbrink and Martin Geiger. Osnabrück, Germany: Institut für Migrationsforschung und Interkulturelle Studien (IMIS)-Beiträge.

Gemenne, François (2011): "Why the Numbers Don't Add Up: A Review of Estimates and Predictions of People Displaced by Environmental Changes", in: Global Environmental Change, 21(1), pp. 41–49. https://doi.org/10.1016/ j.gloenvcha.2011.09.005

Greiner, Clemens/Sakdapolrak, Patrick (2013): "Translocality: Concepts, Applications and Emerging Research Perspectives", in: Geography Compass 7 (5), pp. 373–384. https://doi.org/10.1111/gec3.12048

Jacobson, Jodi L. (1988): "Environmental Refugees: A Yardstick of Habitability", in: Bulletin of Science, Technology & Society 8(3), pp. 257–258. https://doi.org/10.1177/027046768800800304

Kelly, Philip F. (2011): "Migration, Agrarian Transition, and Rural Change in Southeast Asia", in: Critical Asian Studies, 43(4), pp. 479–506. https:// doi.org/10.1080/14672715.2011.623516

Naruchaikusol, Sopon (2016): Climate Change and Its Impact in Thailand: A Short Overview on Actual and Potential Impacts of the Changing Climate in Southeast Asia. TransRe Fact Sheet No. 2, Department of Geography, University of Bonn, Bonn, June 2016. Available online.

Peth, Simon Alexander/Sakdapolrak, Patrick (2020): When the Origin Becomes the Destination: Lost Remittances and Social Resilience of Return Labour Migrants in Thailand", in: Area 52(3), pp. 547–557. https://doi. org/10.1111/area.12598

Peth, Simon Alexander/Sterly, Harald/Sakdapolrak, Patrick (2018): "Between the Village and the Global City: The Production and Decay of Translocal Spaces of Thai Migrant Workers in Singapore", in: Mobilities 13(4), p. 455–472. https://doi.org/10.1080/17450101.2018.1449785

Porst, Luise/Sakdapolrak, Patrick (2018): "Advancing Adaptation or Produc-
    ing Precarity? The Role of Rural-Urban Migration and Translocal Embed-
    dedness in Navigating Household Resilience in Thailand", in: Geoforum
    97, p. 35–45. https://doi.org/10.1016/j.geoforum.2018.10.011

Sakdapolrak, Patrick/Naruchaikusol, Sopon/Ober, Kayly/Peth, Simon/Porst,
    Luise et al. (2016): "Migration in a Changing Climate: Towards a Translocal
    Social Resilience Approach", in: Die Erde 147(2), pp. 81–94. https://doi.org/
    10.12854/erde-147-6

Sterly, Harald/Ober, Kayly/Sakdapolrak, Patrick (2016): "Migration for Hu-
    man Security? The Contribution of Translocality to Social Resilience", in:
    Georgetown Journal of Asian Affairs, 3(1): 57–66. Available online.

United Nations Department of Economic and Social Affairs (UNDESA), Pop-
    ulation Division (2019): International Migrant Stock 2019. Available on-
    line.

United Nations Development Program (UNDP) (2009): Human Development
    Report 2009, Overcoming Barriers: Human Mobility and Development.
    New York: UNDP. Available online.

Contributors

Afeworki Abay, Robel is a research associate at the Institute of Sociology at Ludwig-Maximilians-University of Munich, Germany. His research and teaching interests include: Intersectional Disability Justice; Critical Migration and Mobility; Postcolonial and Decolonial Theories; Climate and Social Justice; Participatory Research.

De Silva, Malith, Junior Researcher, Federation of Sri Lankan Local Government Authorities (FSLGA), Colombo, Sri Lanka. Research areas: municipal solid waste management, discourse analysis, children as a vulnerable group, displacement and relocation.

Donlic, Jasmin, Dr., Assistant Professor at the Department of Educational Science, University of Klagenfurt, Austria; Working Unit for General Pedagogy and Diversity Education. Main research interests: postmigration, diversity and education and qualitative research methods (grounded theory and participatory research).

Fernando, Nishara, Dr., University Professor at the Department of Sociology, University of Colombo, Sri Lanka. Research areas: displacement and relocation, marginalized youth and institutionalized children, natural hazards and resilient communities.

Hollenbach, Pia, Dr., Senior Researcher at the Faculty of Civil Engineering, University of Applied Sciences, Konstanz, Germany. Research areas: post-disaster urban rehabilitation and reconstruction, social dimension(s) of post-disaster urban reconstruction and rehabilitation; community-organized disaster governance, national and international social work and disasters; transnational diaspora studies; sustainable urbanization (bottom-up approaches); solution-oriented research for development.

Huber, Ingrid, Mag., educator at Ingeborg Bachmann Gymnasium, Klagenfurt, Austria; external lecturer in subject didactics at the Institute for Geography and Regional Research, University of Klagenfurt. Teacher of mathematics, geography and economics.

Ibrahim, Fazeela, Dr., Research Associate at Villa College, Malé, Republic of Maldives; main areas of research: migration, social demography, social mobility, life-course perspectives and international higher education in Maldives and Australia.

Ionesco, Dina, Senior Advisor on migration to the Climate Vulnerable Forum (CVF) and Vulnerable 20 Group (V20) and Co-Director of the Masters in Migration, Climate Change and Environment at Webster University, Geneva, Switzerland. Main areas of expertise: migration and climate change in vulnerable countries, education and outreach on migration and climate change.

Kanzian, Horst, Mag., Senior Lecturer at the Institute for Geography and Regional Research at the University of Klagenfurt, Austria. Research interests: media and geomedia in the classroom and in out-of-school places of learning; inter- and transcultural learning with media access; reflective practice in the schools context.

Kromp-Kolb, Helga, PhD, emeritus university professor at the University of Natural Resources and Life Sciences, Vienna, Austria. Fields of work: climate change, atmospheric pollutant dispersion, transforming of universities and society to achieve sustainable development. Focuses: networking, research coordination and policy, knowledge transfer.

Krüger, Marco, Dr., Research Associate at the International Center for Ethics in the Sciences and Humanities (IZEW), University of Tuebingen, Germany. Research areas: (critical) security studies, resilience, surveillance studies, gender and security, science and technology studies.

Mach, Eva, Head of Environmental Sustainability, International Organization for Migration (IOM) Headquarters. Main areas of expertise: clean energy in displacement settings, water and migration.

Peterlini, Hans Karl, Dr., Professor at the Department of Educational Science, University of Klagenfurt, Austria, working in the fields of General Pedagogy and Diversity Education, as well as peace research and peace education. Research interests: personal and social learning processes in schools and lifeworlds, experiences of living together in migration societies, and between majorities and minorities.

Sakdapolrak, Patrick, Dr. is a Professor and leader of the Working Group for Population Geography and Demography at the University of Vienna and a Research Scholar at the International Institute of Applied Systems Analysis (IIASA) in Laxenburg, Austria. He focuses on the intersection of population dynamics, environmental change and development processes, with a focus on the topics of migration and displacement, health and disease.

Sterly, Harald, Dr. is a Senior Scientist at the University of Vienna's Department of Geography and Regional Research, Austria. He studies spatial and social aspects of the intersection of climate and environmental change and different forms of mobility and migration. He is specifically interested in how migration and translocal connectivities affect people's scope for agency, their vulnerability and their resilience.

Schmitt, Caroline, Prof. Dr. phil. habil., is a professor of migration and inclusion research at Klagenfurt University, Austria and a certified diversity educator. Her research and teaching interests include diversity and inclusion in postmigration society; disaster and climate crisis research; solidarity and social movements; transnational and international social work. Contact: https://www.caroline-schmitt.eu/

Schraven, Benjamin is a consultant, migration expert and Associate Fellow of the German Institute for Development and Sustainability (IDOS). He holds a PhD in development studies from the University of Bonn. Benjamin Schraven has advised, among others, the European Union, the World Bank, the International Organization for Migration (IOM) and various UN agencies on issues of flight and migration.

Schmelz, Andrea Frieda, Dr., Professor of International Social Work and Global Development at Coburg University of Applied Sciences and Arts, Germany. Main current research areas: international social work; global migration studies and human rights; green social work & the Anthropocene; transformation research & disaster studies; decolonial memory culture and international social work history.

Traore Chazalnoel, Mariam, Senior Policy Officer at the International Organization for Migration (IOM) Headquarters. Main areas of expertise: global migration governance and climate change, migration in climate change negotiations.

Wilmsen, Brooke, Dr., Senior Lecturer at the School of Humanities and Social Sciences at La Trobe University, Australia. Main areas of research: forced displacement, involuntary resettlement, climate change adaptation, social protection and agrarian change.

GPSR Authorized Representative: Easy Access System Europe, Mustamäe tee
50, 10621 Tallinn, Estonia, gpsr.requests@easproject.com

www.ingramcontent.com/pod-product-compliance
Lightning Source LLC
Chambersburg PA
CBHW070121030426
42335CB00016B/2227